# Flying Free

## Life Lessons Learned on the Flying Trapeze

Lynn Braz

*FLYING FREE:*
*Life Lessons Learned on the Flying Trapeze*

Copyright © 2013 by Lynn Braz

Published by Research Publications, Inc.

For more information about the author:
lynnbraz.com

Book Cover Design:
Trinka Ravaioli
Photo credit:
Jane Richey

ISBN-13: 9780615864327
ISBN-10: 0615864325

# Flying Free: Life Lessons Learned on the Flying Trapeze

"*Flying Free* is one of those books to keep by your bed and pick up for daily inspiration on how to face fears, keep going and conquer whatever it is that stops you from fulfilling your dreams. A fun and easy read."

~ E. Katherine Kerr, Award-winning stage and film actor who costarred in *Silkwood, Children of a Lesser God, Suspect,* among many others. She is also the author of *The Four Principles: Applying the Keys of Brilliant Acting to Life*

"Lynn Braz offers trapeze as a meaningful metaphor for living with honesty that inspires us to leap from our own safe platforms."

~ Erin Byrne, Award-winning author, poet, essayist and filmmaker, whose work has appeared in numerous anthologies and magazines and whose film, *The Storykeeper,* won Best Documentary Short at the 2013 Geneva Film Festival

"In *Flying Free,* Lynn Braz did what the great yogis advise: She went toward her fear instead of running away from it and shows us by example how to extract both practical and profound insights from any activity—particularly those that challenge us. Thank you, Lynn, for daring to let go and fly between the trapeze bars!"

~ Jane Brunette, Author of *Grasshopper Guru,* poet, writing coach, Huffington Post spirituality blogger and founder of global writing circle Writing from the Soul

"Lynn Braz writes with honesty and insight. *Flying Free* inspires us to move past perfectionism and soar."

~ Erin Reese, Author of *The Adventures of Bindi Girl: Diving Deep Into the Heart of India*

"*Flying Free* contains wisdom, spunk, and is written with sincerity. I know of Lynn's fearlessness, as she coached me through mine. The take away I get from reading *Flying Free* is that I can move freely in this world and not be afraid of fear itself. This book is a powerful metaphor and great medicine for these times."

~ J. Delfina Piretti, M.A., M.F.T., psychotherapist and expressive arts therapist

"Lynn writes with awareness and clarity about the joys of transforming challenges into opportunities for richer life experiences."

~ Tarra Christoff, M.A., Creator of the Inspired Work telecast and Omega Institute workshop leader

# Contents

# Introduction

"If you were born without wings, do nothing to prevent them from growing."
— Coco Chanel

*I stand on a narrow platform, twenty-five feet—the height of a two-story build-ing—in the air. Although it's cold in the gym—a converted metal warehouse that refuses to warm—my palms are sweaty, beads of cool sweat dampen my face. I look down at a huge safety net running the entire length and width of the trapeze rig. The net seems hundreds of feet below me. Standing high on my toes, I reach out and grasp a trapeze bar, taking deep breaths to steady my nerves, dimly aware that without consciously breathing I might hyperventilate. The gym is utterly silent while all eyes are on me. It's my first time flying out of lines; that is, after several months of taking flying trapeze classes twice a week, I'm finally ready to swing without the safety lines. Today, for the first time, I'm flying free.*

Flying free—the freedom and thrill and terror of flying—is that elusive moment of being in the zone, when time slows down to something so real and relaxed I can almost grasp it. Nothing can compare to flying, arcing through the air at roughly twenty-five miles an hour, weightless and unrestrained, focused, joyful, wholly in the moment. No worries, no gravity, no limits.

In the San Francisco Bay Area, flying trapeze is not an unusual hobby. Three flying trapeze schools, all within fifty miles of each other, do brisk business. I was in my early forties when I took up trapeze, an age that is fairly average among trapeze hobbyists. What makes trapeze an odd choice for how I spend my leisure time is not my age, nor my lack of acrobatic prowess, nor my relatively sluggish reflexes. Trapeze is a strange choice for me because of my fear of heights.

Terror, actually. My fear of heights has made climbing a ladder to change a light bulb nearly impossible. Driving across a bridge was inconceivable. When attempting to ski as a teenager, the bunny slope may as well have been Mt. Everest. Height was never my friend.

Through trapeze, my fear of heights has been transformed. Fear no longer paralyzes me. Fear no longer scares me.

Trapeze taught me how to face fears and move forward. It helped me learn to trust, let go and focus. Trapeze helped me develop patience, momentum, intention and grace. Trapeze strengthened my discipline, tenacity, integrity and humility (not to mention my spine, triceps, lats and abdominal muscles). Trapeze blessed me with community and courage.

Daily, I apply the lessons I learned from flying trapeze to my life on the ground. Flying trapeze is the hardest, scariest and, yet, most fun thing I've ever done. After trapeze, everything else seems easier. But my appreciation of what I've achieved on the trapeze goes much deeper than pure pleasure. Trapeze became a form of somatic therapy for me, a powerful method for self-discovery, for taking actions to overcome my limitations. Motivated by pure, primal enthusiasm, trapeze became my greatest tool for making real changes in my life.

Through trapeze, I rediscovered dormant passions, the childlike absorption in an activity that feeds my soul. I've since been able to bring that level of energy to numerous other endeavors: travel, relationships, my once-stalled writing career. Trapeze helps me remember how to take calculated risks and stretch beyond my comfort zone to reach new goals. I realized a level of resiliency in trapeze that feeds my self-confidence and helps me remember that I'm stronger than I think. Most importantly, trapeze taught me the value of community, that life's difficulties are much more manageable when I have the support of like-minded friends and colleagues. Trapeze showed me how fun, for fun's sake, can lead to a more fulfilling, successful life.

Flying trapeze set me free.

In *Flying Free*, I share what I've learned through my triumphs and falls on the flying trapeze. It's my hope that *Flying Free* inspires readers to soar to new heights in their own lives, uncovering hidden passions and finding greater joy. **Flying Free is not about learning trapeze. It's about finding a path to transformation that works for you.** Trapeze just happened to be my vehicle. The principles I learned can be gleaned from any activity—from exciting and adventurous, to inevitable and mundane. Anything that makes you stop and take notice of the resistance that arises when you face challenges offers valuable life lessons, if you are willing to learn.

*one*

# Fun Is on the Other Side of Fear

"What difference do it make if the thing you scared of is real or not?"
— Toni Morrison (*Song of Solomon*)

*Standing on the platform, preparing to fly, I go through my usual preflight ritu-*
*als, chalking and re-chalking my hands far more times than necessary, adjust-*
*ing my homemade gauze handgrips and my ponytail, swinging the bar to myself*
*once, twice, three times. I realize in the moment before I hear "Hep" (trapeze talk*
*for "Go") from the flying trapeze catcher, Hans—the sinewy, strong guy on the*
*other trapeze bar, whose job is to catch me after I release my trick, swing me and*
*return me to my own trapeze bar—that something is not quite right. My mind*
*races to identify why this turn at the trapeze, this moment, is utterly different*
*from all the others I've experienced so far. And then I realize: for the first time in*
*trapeze class, I am not scared.*

I've always been fearful, not just of heights. I was the kind of kid
who was afraid of getting hurt, too scared to try anything new, shunning roller coasters, Ferris wheels and go-carts in favor of a slow-moving
merry-go-round. And even that gave me the willies if my mom wasn't
holding my hand. If it were up to me, I'd probably have opted to keep
the training wheels on my bike until I was in high school. I'd watch
other kids gleefully attempt what seemed like dangerous activities—
scampering over logs strewn across streams, swinging from monkey

1

bars, climbing trees—and wished I could be like them. My fears held me back from trying and, when I did manage to push past the fear, fear kept me from enjoying myself.

Trying the flying trapeze seemed utterly ridiculous. I was on a Club Med vacation and one of the activities at many Club Meds is flying trapeze. Let me say this straight off: flying trapeze, at least at the beginner level, is a safe activity. More Club Med vacationers are injured playing ping pong than trying trapeze. The beginner flyer always wears safety lines and, of course, there's always a net. At Club Med, watching other ordinary people try the trapeze was an interesting undertaking for me. While no one looked as scared as I felt, most people definitely did not seem fearless. Some quivered climbing the ladder, some were scared just standing on the platform, some seemed frightened to try the first trick every beginner is taught—the knee hang. Some balked at letting go of the bar and falling to the net. I assume there were even some like me—petrified of the entire process.

I felt compelled to try trapeze anyway. The introductory trick, the knee hang, does not require physical ability; it's the most simple trick. I'd had years of training in ballet, yoga and Pilates. I knew I was physically qualified to attempt the knee hang. The only thing that would prevent me from doing it would be my fear.

Practicing the knee hang on a bar a mere nine feet off the ground made me feel anxious. Climbing the ladder truly terrified me. Standing on the platform, I felt as if I was going to have a stroke. I'd watched at least fifty other people—some with beer guts and butts that had never been subjected to a yoga class—go ahead of me and not one of them climbed back down the ladder. I knew the only way down was to first fly high.

I stood on the tiny, narrow platform high in the air with the flying trapeze instructor urging me to rise onto the balls of my feet. A slight sea breeze stirred, blowing pieces of hair into my eyes. Salt mixed with the metallic taste of fear in my mouth. I could smell the instructor's sweat and hair gel. Fear coursed throughout my entire body. I felt lightheaded, on the verge of throwing up. I nervously chatted up the instructor, a young man from Mexico who didn't speak much English. The instructors on the ground grew impatient with me, urging me to grasp the fly bar, stand up straight. "Ready. Hep!" they commanded, which is trapeze for, "Shut up and fly."

I'd like to say the second time I flew I felt less fear, but that's not true. Back in the Bay Area, for a few months, I felt intense fear every time I climbed that ladder. Even now as an experienced flyer, I still feel fear; it's lessened considerably, but it's there nonetheless. The biggest difference is that I've become comfortable with the discomfort of fear. I've redefined the significance of fear. I've become friendly with fear.

Developing a healthy relationship with fear required a multifaceted approach. It required discipline and discernment. For months in flying trapeze class, I'd feel my fear and my head would scream, "Oh no! I'm scared again. How can I still be scared? Why am I still scared? What's wrong with me?" I'd look around the class—no one else seemed or sounded fearful. I'd constantly tell everyone I was afraid, which continued to affirm the fear to myself. One day I told a classmate, Sue, that my heart rate started to rise even before I got in my car to drive to class. "Me, too," Sue laughed. She said she was relieved to hear she wasn't the only one who'd been flying for months and was still afraid.

Knowing I wasn't unique in my fear helped me feel less freaked out. Sue and I started joking about our fear. I learned that talking about fear with Sue was safe because she understood and didn't judge me for being afraid. Some of the other students and most of the instructors were not as compassionate. Not having experienced fear to the extent I had, they didn't understand my terror. They kept saying things like, "You've done this before. You're wearing safety lines. Why are you afraid?" Their judgments made me feel worse.

I learned there is a fine line between sharing my feelings, which can help alleviate the pain of the uncomfortable feeling and *feeding* my uncomfortable feelings. Telling everyone in the gym I was scared fed the fear. Repeatedly telling my instructors I was frightened and trying to make it their job to make me feel less so, also fed the fear. On the other hand, sharing my feelings honestly with one other person and then letting go of the topic, helped assuage my fear. I learned that anytime I wanted someone else to change my feelings—usually fear or anxiety—I was merely further empowering the fear. Whenever I tried to make someone else responsible for how I felt, I felt worse. It was the intention behind my sharing my feelings that determined whether talking about those feelings helped or hurt me.

There came a point when I had to decide if I wanted to continue with a hobby that scared me. Does it make sense to do something two or three times a week that brings out intense fear? Was the incredible adrenaline rush (euphoria, really) that I felt at the end of class worth walking (or, in this case, flying) through all that fear during class? I started bargaining with myself, "If I'm still afraid tonight in class, this is going to be my last class." Bargaining worked for that one class—it seemed like I was a lot less fearful. Until the next class, and there I was again, scared silly. Then every class became a wavering wishy-washy endeavor. "Maybe I'll quit. Maybe I'll just stick with beginner tricks. Maybe I'll just do a little bit and leave early. Maybe I'll go late and take it real easy," I would say to myself. What I realized is that I hadn't fully committed to my hobby. I was always giving myself an out. "If I don't feel like it, I don't have to do it" became my mantra.

That attitude is not good for any relationship and it certainly wasn't good for my relationship with fear. Knowing when to take it easy—participating in an adventure sport when I'm not feeling well or I'm sleep-deprived or injured is unwise. But my wavering before every class fed my fear. The message to my subconscious was clear: fear is the biggest thing in my life because it's getting most of my attention. Fear is bigger than a sport I love and am becoming pretty good at. Fear is bigger than the friendships I've formed. Fear is bigger than having fun. Fear was winning because I wasn't committed to relating to it in a healthy way: acknowledging it, thanking it for its diligent caution and then putting my attention where it needed to be—on having fun.

Not dwelling on fear has created a much healthier relationship with it. Now, when I feel fearful I no longer tell everyone within earshot that I'm scared. I no longer try to foist off my uncomfortable feelings on others and make it their responsibility to change the way I feel. When fear comes up, I acknowledge it and then put it aside and do what I need to do. Sometimes I thank my fear, which is very prudent. What I'm doing is potentially dangerous. I'm flying through the air, often no longer wearing safety lines because I'm advanced enough to swing and do certain tricks without them. Fear is a reasonable response. Fear is a healthy, normal feeling that reminds me to stay focused on what I'm doing and to make good split-second decisions. Fear is sometimes a signal that something is not quite right. Fear can be an honest, helpful emotion.

But it can also be a liar. Fear will tell me I don't deserve to pursue my dreams or I'm too old, too limited, not smart enough, not attractive enough or just plain not enough. Fear can masquerade as perfectionism, the need to do things perfectly or not at all. Fear can also masquerade as anger or sadness.

I don't always know when my fear is warranted and helpful and when my fear is just an illusion keeping me from soaring to new heights. I can rationalize ("rational lies") doing or not doing anything based on fear. Navigating fear requires the ability to connect with my deep, inner truth—which can be just as frightening as stepping off a platform and into the air.

Something one of the trapeze instructors said to me was pivotal in redefining my relationship to fear. "Flying trapeze is an exciting sport," Hans said. "Fear and excitement feel a lot alike. Maybe you're just excited."

I had an excellent opportunity to test this theory while backpacking through the Indian Himalayas alone during the winter of 2007. The destination that topped my travel wish list, Kashmir, was considered dangerous because of terrorism. Emails from a guide in Kashmir's ski village, Gulmarg, confirmed the latest rounds of attacks a month earlier in Srinagar, the city in which the airport is situated. While in Darjeeling, I learned Gulmarg lies a mere three miles from the line of control between Pakistan and India, one of the most volatile spots in the region.

Every time I considered canceling my trip to Gulmarg I thought about trapeze. How scary it was for me to face my fears and fly anyway, and how rewarding an experience it's been. I decided to follow through with traveling to Kashmir.

Thankfully.

The things I remember most about my experience include the Kashmiris' amazing generosity and hospitality and how, as the only single woman to visit the village, I was treated like a queen, escorted to and from restaurants and Internet cafés as if I was the most important person in the world. Space heaters were dragged over to me each time I entered the ski lodge. Watching the scene that surrounded me everywhere I went in Gulmarg, a Swedish man asked, "So, how does it feel to be a goddess?" The skiing was also amazing—twenty-three kilometers of off-piste powder, slopes surrounded by twenty-thousand-foot peaks that soared above the clouds, views for miles deep into the valleys, all the way to Pakistan.

Locals constantly commented on how brave I was. I had to chuckle at that. What I learned is that facing my biggest fear gave me courage and the most fun week of my life. Fun is on the other side of fear.

* * *

# two

# You're Stronger Than You Think

"It is really wonderful how much resilience there is in human nature."
— Bram Stoker (*Dracula*)

*I'm lying face down, crumpled in the net, the result of my angel return, the new trick I'm learning, gone wrong. To execute the angel return after being caught by the catcher, instead of swinging with him and performing a half-turn back to my own fly bar, I lift my legs up to the catcher's shoulders. He grabs one of my legs, the other one drops down toward the net as the catcher turns me over so that I'm in an arabesque position. He's holding one of my arms and one of my legs. Done well, this simple—yet beautiful—trick looks like a ballerina dancing through the air. Unfortunately, I've yet to do it well.*

*Right before hitting the net, I hear the catcher blurt out a shaky, "Whoa," as he drops me. The collective gasp from everyone else in the gym who happens to be watching my trick isn't exactly comforting. The instructor on the ground asks if I need an ambulance. Adrenaline, a natural pain killer, pumps through me, yet I know I'm not injured. Pushing myself up gingerly, I crawl out of the net to a chorus of worried voices asking if I'm okay. I hear my friend Shannon say, "Nice net burn." Every uncovered part of the left side of my body, including my face, is bruised.*

*"Get back up there right now," Janene, the instructor, orders.*

*"Absolutely not," I say with finality. Defying Janene is not something I do. I'm more afraid of her—in a good way—than I am of heights. I try to sit down.*

*"If you can walk, you can fly. Get. Back. Up. There. Now!"*

*My classmates nod in agreement. Sharon, the friend I've known the longest, who has been flying for years, calls down to me. "Come on, Lynnie. You've got to go again or you may never go again."*

*I want to learn the angel return. For my upcoming forty-fifth birthday, I'm throwing myself a party, replete with a flying trapeze performance starring me and three trapeze friends: Cory, Mitchell and Shannon. The splits position catch to an angel return is my planned* pièce de résistance. *Not mastering the trick is not an option. Motivated by sheer vanity, instead of telling myself my old trapeze story—I'm scared—I try a new tactic to avoid panicking. "Okay," I remind myself. "The worst that could happen just happened. And you're fine. Just a little bumped up, but otherwise fine." I'm actually talking to myself out loud.*

*"Just do the trick right and you'll be okay," Janene chimes in.*

*I'm understandably shaky as I grab the trapeze bar and call, "Listo," which is trapeze—and Spanish—for "Ready." I force a smile in an attempt to fool myself into thinking I'm happy. I hear the catcher call, "Ready. Hep."*

*I jump off the board. I really don't remember anything else, except that I ended up back on my own return bar, where I belong, without incident.*

I can't tell you how many times I've done—and seen—things in trapeze class that look as if paramedics should be on the scene: flyers bouncing out of the net after a fall, flyers twisting violently off the bar when attempting to return to the platform, a flyer pulling the catcher off his trapeze bar with a bad trick and ill-advised catch, and flyer and catcher colliding as they bounced in the net. I've seen numerous falls to the net: head first, face first, and feet first—all of which were chilling to witness. I watched my friend Shannon perform one of the trickier tricks, a forward over, in which she swings out and pulls herself up onto the bar, resting on her hips. She releases the bar and executes a front somersault over it, extending her arms for the catch. Battling a stomach virus one day, Shannon's timing a hair off, she slipped off the bar, which flew back into her face, breaking her nose. When the bleeding stopped, she got back on the trapeze and tried the trick again. That second attempt was flawless.

Life can seem so tenuous at times, anyone could be pardoned for believing humans are fragile creatures easily shattered by illness and accidents and numerous natural forces beyond our control. As further illustration of our inherent vulnerability, we can look at the global financial downturns and the alarming ease with which assets and pensions and mortgages can crumble. If you've lost a loved one, especially to an untimely or sudden death, you know not to take anything about life and wellness and security for granted.

And yet, we humans are a hearty lot. In trapeze I am constantly amazed by the human resilience I experience and witness regularly.

My resilience in life outside of trapeze has been put to the test in recent years. The evolution of publishing—changes which I failed to prepare for—dealt heavy economic blows to my editorial business in the years since 2008. I cobbled together a dramatically-reduced income with part-time jobs supplementing my freelance work. Coming close to conceding it was time to move on, I considered perhaps heading back to school for retraining in another field. But each time I seriously contemplated giving up on writing, I visualized that angel return. I remembered what one of my coaches, Darrell, said to me when I thought I was too weak, too beaten to attempt another trick I found difficult and frustrating: "You're stronger than you think."

I realized that is also true of my mental and emotional toughness.

One of the most important applications of resilience in real life arises in relationships. A romance gone wrong or a broken friendship can create a world of mistrust and fear of connecting. How many of us have been through heartache so devastating that we thought we'd never feel joy again? And yet, with time and willingness, we not only heal, but go on to enjoy even greater happiness and fulfillment in subsequent relationships.

The belief that I'm fragile and easily hurt caused me to avoid many potentially wonderful possibilities. I could not view any setback as just a bump in the road. Every glitch was a sign to quit, break up or run away. Lack of knowledge of my resilience caused me to play small and underperform in a variety of situations. "If I don't take risks," I reasoned, "I will never be in peril." I didn't realize back then that resilience was part of the human conditioning. Yes, tragedies occur and humans are not immortal. We are also not gossamer. Our bodies, minds, emotions and spirits have an inherent healing ability. Falls, drops, losses, breakups, progressing age, even illness, do not necessarily mean you can't go on to future successes.

You are stronger than you think.

* * *

# *three*

# Raising the Energy

"The greatest weariness comes from work not done."
— Eric Hoffer

*It's early Tuesday morning; I drag myself to trapeze class despite intense sleep deprivation and the accompanying torpid, fog-headed blahs. My trapeze classes are paid in advance and even though I don't think I'm physically capable of doing much, I figure even one turn is better than totally wasting my money. Besides, maybe I'll learn something from watching my classmates. By the time I reach the gym, I regret my decision to show up. I plop down next to my instructor, Stephan Gaudreau, and tell him I'm just going to stretch out on the practice bar and skip the flying part of trapeze today.*

*"Put on a belt and take a warm-up swing," Stef suggests. The safety belt ensures that if I do fall asleep in midair, he can safely lower me to the net.*

*I comply. While trying a trick seems inconceivable, there's no risk in merely doing a warm-up swing wearing safety lines. I step off the platform warily, moving with little exertion, stretching into an arch, which loosens the knots in my shoulders and clears my mind a bit. Warming up in the air feels so good that I go for a second turn. I still don't put in much effort and I am still too tired for a proper swing, but I enjoy its gentle—albeit halfhearted—motion and feel my body start to come alive. I climb the ladder a third time, then a fourth time. Halfway through the class, I realize I'm alert and my body feels strong. I'm swinging with enough oomph to throw tricks. By the end of class, I'm catching my tricks, the listless start to my trapeze experience completely transformed.*

In trapeze, most tricks begin with a swing. The bigger the swing, the better the trick. The energy of the swing allows the flyer to gain height and momentum so that, when she releases to the catcher, she can "float" smoothly and naturally to him. If her swing doesn't have enough energy, the catcher will have to extend toward her and pull her in. Even though the swing is not the most glamorous part of the trick—it might even seem like something that has to be gotten out of the way—it is the foundation of the whole performance, because that is where the flyer builds the energy needed to execute well. The momentum generated in the earliest stages of the trick carries through to the end, making every part of the trick better, from the release to the catcher, to the return landing on the platform.

Building energy means starting where you are, taking one action, and continuing to take action, whether you feel like it or not. We can all think of things we've started, only to run out of steam a short time later. Every project, idea, hobby and life goal needs a steady stream of energy to feed and sustain it. The ability to build energy is crucial to success in every area of life. If you've done your groundwork—the arduous, unglamorous tasks—with energy, you'll be in a good position when your big moment comes. Caring as much about the mundane elements of every endeavor as you do about the more exciting aspects imbues any undertaking with vitality.

Investing energy produces more energy. With physical activity, the energy you put into a workout makes you stronger, which gives you more energy. How often are you sitting at your desk, writing emails or surfing the Internet for information you don't really need when you know you would benefit much more from going for a jog or taking a yoga class?

Think about your own experience with exercise. No matter how tired you feel when you walk into the gym or yoga studio, you can count on feeling better when you walk out, if only for the fact that you know you did something good for yourself. The action shifts your energy.

Mental and emotional energies work under the same principles as physical energies: when we put energy into worthwhile tasks—whether or not those tasks are fun and exciting—we feel good about our work and we become habituated to building and using energy. How often do you procrastinate in starting something and find that it becomes even more difficult to get going? Jumping in—even when you don't feel like it—can be energizing.

There is a well-known adage: you cannot think yourself into right action, but you can act yourself into right thinking. Taking an action, no matter how small, gets the energy moving in the right direction. Building energy in one area of life can spill into other areas of life.

Leigh Anne was thirty-three years old when she took her first trapeze class. She was suffering from Crohn's disease—a chronic inflammatory disease of the intestines that can also affect the digestive system—and weighed less than 90 pounds. After a lengthy hospitalization and an ileostomy, Leigh Anne's doctor told her to find an enjoyable low-impact exercise to help her build strength. At that time she was physically and emotionally compromised, but she chose trapeze because it was such an unlikely choice, and she felt she needed to do something dramatic to help her get her life back on track.

Leigh Anne says initially she looked forward to the excitement of class, despite having little natural ability. After a few swings, she'd land in the net, visibly shaking. But, encouraged by her instructors, she stuck with it, and the adrenaline rush of flying helped ease the depression brought on by the disease and long convalescence.

Because of her illness, Leigh Anne had been accustomed to having no appetite and to feeling exhausted, especially after working an eight-hour day as a hotel concierge. After trapeze classes, however, she felt energized and found her appetite began increasing. She'd eat a big meal and keep a peanut butter sandwich on her nightstand for a late-night snack. Within a few months of trapeze twice a week, Leigh Anne had gained fifteen pounds and, after a year, she began performing. "Taking trapeze class began the process of rebuilding my self-confidence, very gradually," Leigh Anne says. "After my surgery, it was hard to function. It was difficult to work an eight-hour day. Once I started trapeze, I got stronger and my everyday life got easier. I constantly marvel at how this has turned my life around."

There may be times when it's impossible to build energy on your own. You may need to "borrow" energy by drawing on the collective group energy available through your community, family, friends and colleagues. There are times when I show up for trapeze class feeling tired and low-energy. Fortunately, trapeze instructors and flyers are energetic people; if I let myself be open and responsive to their enthusiasm, I feel a boost.

In the world outside trapeze, I've learned to "bookend" difficult tasks by calling someone I can rely on for support and telling him or her what my intention is, which helps me build momentum for the task. I call again once I've taken an action towards that intention, which affirms that I am determined and able to follow through with my goals. The action of placing that initial phone call is often the first step towards upping my energetic reserves.

Using breath is one of the most powerful and simple ways to increase energy. One way to wake up physically and mentally is to practice a basic yogic breathing exercise—*kapalabhati* breathing, or "breath of fire."

To practice this ancient breathing technique, sit comfortably and close your eyes. Bring your attention to your breath and simply observe it flowing in and out. Quietly observe for a few breaths. When you are ready, take three long, deep breaths, focusing on the exhale. On the third breath, hold your breath in and, keeping your mouth closed, begin pumping the breath out of your nostrils, using your diaphragm. Allow the next inhale to happen naturally; then bring your attention to the exhale while pumping the breath, slowly at first.

Once you've become comfortable with breathing this way, begin increasing the speed of your breaths. Only your breath and abdominal muscles should be moving. Everything else in the body remains stationary.

When beginning this breathing practice, start with thirty breaths and build up, over time, to the point where you can continue *kapalabhati* breathing for two to three minutes (use an alarm clock or kitchen timer). Allow your last inhalation to be long and deep, and hold in the breath for a count of sixty, noticing how much oxygen you've created in your body through *kapalabhati* breathing. Remain sitting for a minute or two after this exercise to allow your breathing to return to normal. *Kapalabhati* breathing can help clear the mind, which helps the body feel energized.

Our bodies, minds and emotions are all subject to the same laws of physics as the entire universe: an object at rest stays at rest and an object in motion stays in motion. Energy begets energy and regardless of how low you feel, you can always build energy.

\* \* \*

# *four*
# Silencing Self-Doubt

"Our doubts are traitors, and make us lose the good we oft might win,
by fearing to attempt."
— William Shakespeare (*Measure for Measure*)

*"Time to learn something new," Stef says to me on an evening when both he and I were sick of my doing the same two tricks over and over. "Time to learn the turnaround. Grab a twisty belt."*

*Oh, the enigmatic twisty belt. It reminded me of a giant version of the retainer I wore as a kid back in the Sixties—a huge metal contraption that extended a good three inches off my face, and was supposed to wrestle my gopher-like front teeth back into my mouth. This trapeze version is a belt with a metal ring extending out from it—think Saturn—that is worn around the waist. It looks clunky and heavy and, perhaps due to my association with the aforementioned retainer, potentially painful, requiring assistance merely to put it on. It also takes up a lot of space on the platform. Watching other flyers use it to learn turning and twisting tricks always made me worry someone would get bumped off the board. But it was time for me to learn the turnaround, so despite my reservations, I wriggled into the cumbersome contraption.*

The turnaround is a gateway skill; mastering it opens up numerous, possibly even infinite options, on the trapeze. To accomplish a turnaround, the flyer swings out and, as the name suggests, turns around so that she is flying back towards the platform, facing the platform head on. The turnaround involves re-gripping either one or both hands, which involves letting go of the bar for less than a split second with one or both hands. For the first few months of flying trapeze, any situation in which I was in the air and not hanging on to either the bar or catcher with both hands was an opportunity for panic. That first turnaround was, shall we say, less than graceful, but it worked out more or less the way it was supposed to work out.

When I'm learning a new skill, I often perform it better the first time I try it than I do the second, third, fourth or fourteenth times. For the longest time this made no sense to me, until I realized I was experiencing beginner's luck. Beginner's luck is that blissful state of being too inexperienced to doubt my ability to perform a new trick, a new job or any new activity. Beginner's luck is that brief respite before I crush myself with self-doubt.

The second time I tried the turnaround, I re-gripped, saw the platform, realized I was headed straight for it and continued to stare at it as my body crashed into it, both feet slamming, both ankles jamming, on impact. In flying trapeze, as in life, the body follows the eyes. If I'm looking at the net, chances are I'm headed for it face-first. If I'm looking at the platform, that's where my body will wind up, one way or another.

Most things in trapeze look much easier in the hands of a competent flyer. If I've been watching accomplished flyers perform any given trick, without having witnessed their learning process, I might not realize how complicated the trick is and the skill involved in performing it. I might think the trick is easy and because I think it's easy and the mind is very powerful, the trick *becomes* easy that first time I try it. Then I receive feedback from the instructors about all the ways I can improve for my second attempt and I start to realize, "Damn, this is hard." I climb the ladder and, instead of thinking the trick is easy and despite having done it and experiencing it as easy, I worry I won't be able to do it again. Even though I know that anything I do once, I can do twice, self-doubt courses through my mind and messes with my reality.

After crashing into the platform on the second turnaround attempt, I became fearful of both the turnaround *and* the platform. Each subsequent attempt at a turnaround played out the same way. I'd leave the pedestal with a mixed grip (right hand gripping from underneath, left hand in the customary overhand grip), swing out, flail my body into a half turn facing the pedestal, scare the crap out of myself by telling myself, "Don't crash," and then I'd ram right into the platform. Staring at the platform as I was about to crash into it guaranteed I'd do just that. So did telling myself, "Don't crash," since the subconscious mind just hears the word "crash." No matter how many times I tried, I refused to lift my gaze high enough to safely move my legs up and over the pedestal. I doubted my ability to simply lift my legs.

Eventually, after crashing into the pedestal at least a hundred times and compensating for that by wearing enough padding to venture onto a football field and play linebacker as well as trying at least five different versions of the turnaround, I learned to fly facing the platform without crashing into it. I wouldn't say, in this instance, that I overcame self-doubt. I think I just wore it out. I outlasted my self-doubt about the turnaround. Unfortunately, self-doubt is a chameleon; it changes to suit its environment.

Another way self-doubt plays out in trapeze is when I do a trick well ten times in a row and then mess it up on the eleventh try. Maybe I'm tired by the eleventh try. Or maybe it was just a fluke, a slight bobble in my timing or even the instructor's fault. Self-doubt will persuade me to ignore the ten times I performed well and focus all of my (negative) energy on the one time I failed.

Coping with self-doubt requires discipline; I can't let my mind stay focused on what didn't work the last time I did the trick or why I missed my catch. I have to take in the feedback from the instructors, process it and tell myself, "I can do this." Then I have to act as if I believe I can do it, reminding myself that the past does not predict the future.

Often, I do my best when the instructors surprise me. Perhaps I'll be warming up or dropping to the net and an instructor suggests I go into a trick position or do a flip in the net. If he tells me to do this while I'm standing on the platform and I have time to think about it, my self-doubt might creep in. But when I'm told to do something and I don't have time to think about it, I'm usually successful. I try to remember that during those moments when I'm plagued with doubt.

I've seen numerous other flyers—beautiful, talented, proficient flyers—say something self-defeating right before they are about to do a trick. Sometimes the trick works out well anyway, but they sure don't look like they're having much fun. Self-doubt is self-sabotage. If I'm trying to do something, I must on some level believe there's a chance I will do it. Self-doubt is not only self-defeating and a complete killjoy, it's a liar.

Self-doubt, another form of fear, which has hundreds of manifestations, is lethal in every situation. Trapeze drove home the wisdom of ancient Roman poet Virgil: "They can because they think they can." You can succeed at anything you give your honest effort to when you silence self-doubt.

\* \* \*

# *five*

# Unlearning Mistrust

"All the world is made of faith, and trust, and pixie dust."
— J.M. Barrie (*Peter Pan*)

*Still relatively new to trapeze, tonight I am nonetheless being coaxed into trying my first intermediate trick—the layout—which is a straight body somersault. This seems like an utterly futile exercise. Unlike beginner tricks, the layout demands height, of which my less-than-stellar swing gains me little. Also, my still-wonky takeoff often kills any height I might be able to muscle right from the get-go. Yet, I've got to believe my instructors wouldn't suggest I do something unless they think I'm capable, and I've watched my classmates throw literally hundreds of beautiful layouts. I would love to be able to do the same, and I know I've got to start somewhere. I don my trusty safety belt, check and recheck that the carabiners are fastened correctly to the safety lines, chalk my hands for a good two minutes and reach for the bar, calling "Listo."*

*I jump up and to my surprise, my takeoff isn't bad. Encouraged by this, I give my swing everything I have and am again surprised that I've built rather decent height. I draw my legs up, forming an L position with my body, and when I hear the instructor call, "Break!" I drive my legs behind me with all my force. As the trapeze arc pulls me forward and up, my legs float up in front of me. There is a moment—less than a second—where the trapeze bar is completely motionless, when my body is in a handstand position. That's the moment, I hear "Hep!" and release the bar, extending my arms forward.*

*That's how it happened in my imagination. In reality, I released the bar several seconds before the instructor called "Hep" which, because of the forward momentum of the trapeze cables, hurled me forward at a pace of about twenty-five miles per hour, much like one of those circus clowns who is shot out of a cannon. Without the safety lines, it would have been a bad scene. When I got back on the ground, my friend Cory, motioning towards the gallant instructor pulling my safety lines, said to me, "You should thank him. He just saved your life."*

The layout was the first trick I attempted where I had to trust the instructors implicitly. I had to listen to their instructions and do exactly what they said to do when they said to do it. Messing up on my end meant the instructors would literally have to reel me in with the safety lines or I'd most likely hit the net like a bug hitting a windshield, possibly head first. I remember standing on the platform, looking down at the instructor. Since he was not one of my usual teachers, I didn't know him well. As he assured me that I would be safe, I thought about that damn turnaround and how instructors who did know me and my trapeze idiosyncrasies couldn't keep me from crashing into the platform, because safety lines can only do so much if the flyer is determined to screw up. Trusting someone I didn't know and who didn't know me seemed impossible.

Somehow I managed to do just that. I trusted him to teach me the layout and to bail me out if I did it wrong, which I did. By the end of the night, I was catching the trick, which became one of my most exciting trapeze moments. This thrill, this sense of accomplishment, this exhilaration and fun, was only available to me because I was willing to trust.

So much of life is about trusting people we don't know. Every time we get behind the wheel of our car, we are trusting that the other drivers we encounter are competent and that they will do what they are supposed to do. We trust doctors, teachers, hair stylists, restaurant professionals. Daily, we endow someone we don't know with our trust.

Sometimes it's easier to trust strangers than it is our loved ones. Sometimes the more intimate we become with others, the harder it is for us to give them our trust. It makes sense. There is so much more at stake if someone we love betrays our trust.

Trust is singularly the most important skill trapeze develops. Everything else—timing, letting go, patience, staying safe—is based on trust. Often, what the instructors tell us to do sounds counterintuitive. Letting go of the bar can seem like a bad idea, even though it's the only way to accomplish the trick.

In life, the success of all relationships is built on trust. As kids, we have to trust our parents to care for us. We trust our dogs not to bite us. We trust our employers to pay us. At some point our trust is broken and we're faced with the more difficult task of learning to trust someone who's let us down.

In trapeze, if you do what the instructors tell you to do when they tell you to do it, you generally experience a good result. Not always, though. Flying trapeze instructors are human and all humans make mistakes. Early in my trapeze experience I had a bad fall to the net, partly because the instructor didn't bail me out with the safety lines. I knew that if I let that fall inform every other trapeze class I took, I would not be taking trapeze classes for long. I have to admit, I was leery of the instructor for weeks after that fall, but I summoned all of my ability to trust both the instructor and myself. I made an effort to develop a stronger relationship with the instructor so that I wouldn't develop animosity and feel unsafe each time he taught a class I was in. The result is that he is one of my favorite instructors today and has taught me more than anyone else.

When I adopted my first dog in my adulthood, a shih-tzu I named Jersey, I trusted no one with him. I was afraid other dogs would attack. I was afraid the neighbor's two-year-old would rough him up too much. I was afraid if I let him off-leash at the dog park or on the beach, someone would steal him. Jersey and I lived in Manhattan for the first year of his life. I used to take him to Madison Square Park and hold him on my lap as we both watched the other dogs run around and play with each other, doing the kind of things dogs enjoy. Poor Jersey—I wouldn't let the other dogs near him. I balked when someone wanted to pet him. If I could have hired bodyguards for him, I would have. After moving to the Bay Area and taking up trapeze, my vice-like grip on Jersey began to ease. Eventually he enjoyed an almost-normal dog's life, replete with running off-leash, being approached by strangers, even little ruffians, and play dates with other dogs. Jersey was much happier for my relinquishing mistrust, and so was I.

Trapeze taught me that mistrust doesn't serve me. It only keeps me from connecting with people and trying new activities that might bring me joy. No risk, no reward. Being willing to relinquish mistrust is the price I pay for the good things in my life.

\* \* \*

*six*

# Timing Is Everything

"Patience is not passive waiting. Patience is active acceptance of the
process required to attain your goals and dreams."
— Ray Davis

*I sit on top of the trapeze bar, my back arched coquettishly, feeling fabulous. My
new trick, the seat roll, is not often performed here in my gym, which makes me
feel unique—a feeling I enjoy. To accomplish the seat roll, I step off the platform
and curl my legs under the trapeze bar, straightening them out into a pike position. After a full swing in that position, I pop my legs over the bar while pulling
myself up to a seated position. On the call of "Hep," I release my arms and roll
backwards under the bar, arching my back. This is a beautiful trick for me.*

*Throughout the class, I make various mistakes. Sometimes it takes three
swings to get myself up on the bar. Sometimes I rush and fail to get on the bar at
all. There are two moments in trapeze when the flyer is weightless—at the top of
each swing. Popping my legs over the bar when I'm weightless creates an effortless trick. A fraction of a second too soon or too late creates the opposite effect. If
my timing is off, I may still be able to muscle myself up onto the bar, but I kill
any shot I have at a graceful, pretty trick.*

27

*After a full hour of practicing the seat roll without the catcher, I've finally managed to find that sweet spot of weightlessness for moving into trick position. Now it's time to catch the trick with Hans.*

*Turn after turn, I revert to my bad timing: I'm late pulling myself up onto the bar. I need an extra swing to seat myself, which ruins any chance I have of catching the trick. It's the last catch attempt of the night and I've finally regained the sweet spot. I'm seated on the bar, looking (in my mind) positively lovely, waiting for the "Hep," poised for my catch. I arch back, releasing the trapeze cables, rolling gracefully under the bar. Much to my surprise, I fall to the net.*

*"That was the one," my instructor Paris, who is pulling my safety lines, says. "That one was perfect. But then you released the bar too early."*

Successfully accomplishing a trick on the trapeze requires split-second timing. If I am early or late by so much as a single beat, the entire timing of the trick will be off. Sometimes the catcher can compensate for my mistiming by adjusting his swing. Sometimes he can't. With the seat roll, it's nearly impossible for the catcher to bail out my bad timing. Things always work out best when I do the right thing at the right time.

The typical trapeze trick lasts about eighteen seconds from the moment the flyer departs the pedestal to the moment she returns to it. Eighteen seconds pass quickly and, yet, my most common mistake on the trapeze is rushing.

In real life, we're generally told that being early is better than being late. In trapeze, the opposite is true.

Rushing in trapeze is not only ridiculous—the trick is over in the blink of an eye, after all—it's dangerous. At my intermediate trapeze level of ability, most of my tricks are caught by the catcher at a moment when I am motionless. If I rush to make the catch and release the bar early, I'm releasing with forward momentum and putting the catcher at risk for my slamming into him. Even if he can make the catch—and all of my catchers can because they are amazing—I'm still putting him at risk for injuring his shoulders as he catches my wonky trick. So rushing is not only dangerous and silly, it's selfish.

Outside trapeze, rushing is also both dangerous and selfish. If I leave the house late for an appointment and I try to make up the time by rushing in the car, I put myself and all the other drivers on the road at greater risk of accident. Rushing causes me to disconnect from myself and my integrity regarding the activity. Rushing demands that I cut corners, not come to a full stop at stop signs, drive faster than is safe (and legal) and grow impatient with everyone else on the road because they're not adapting their behavior to my agenda.

Sports psychology books talk about being in the zone, a state of consciousness where time slows down and athletes feel as if they are moving in slow motion. Basketball players report the hoop seeming like it's ten feet wide when they're in the zone. Tennis players say they can see the fuzz on the ball before striking it when they're in the zone. I have moments of pure bliss when I'm in the zone and I have many more moments that aren't so blissful when I'm out of the zone. My breathing is shallow, I fail to process vital information, I focus on the wrong details and I rush.

Sometimes my rushing is propelled by fear. Sometimes it's caused by being unable to do the trick slowly. When I haven't created the necessary foundation for an activity and learned how to do the trick step by step, detail by detail, I rush to complete the trick. If I lack the coordination, strength or body awareness to pull my hips up to the bar, I'll compensate by flinging my legs at it. I may accomplish the right result with the wrong technique, but I'll never feel secure doing the trick if I know my foundation is not firm. I may be able to fool the audience into thinking I know what I'm doing, but I can't fool myself. If I don't own the trick, I know it.

Rushing is always a signal something's wrong. If I can't do the skill or activity slowly, I have no business doing it fast. Speed can't make up for lack of skill.

Once I realized how detrimental rushing is in trapeze, I began paying attention to how rushing affected the rest of my life, since rushing was my normal speed. Rushing, I realized, piques my adrenaline and creates anxiety and distraction. Since I know the problem and the solution are never the same thing, I began practicing the antidote to rushing: taking my time, even when I was running late. Instead of driving like a maniac, erratically changing lanes and running yellow lights, I began driving leisurely. What I experienced with my new approach surprised me. I found it took virtually the same amount of time to get somewhere when I moved at a conscious speed as it did when I rushed. The only thing accomplished by rushing was greater anxiety.

Not rushing, like so many things in flying trapeze and in life, is counterintuitive for me. Practicing not rushing taught me that rushing through trapeze diminished my enjoyment of my flight. Rushing through life diminishes my ability to enjoy life.

Developing patience through trapeze has spilled into many other areas of my life. I have a much better ability to tolerate the frustration of waiting in a long supermarket line while the cashier chats up each customer. I've had the patience to spend nearly a year traveling in India, where train and plane and bus departure times are meaningless, where chaos is the norm. If I'd traveled to India with my rushing mentality, I would have had a miserable time; I probably would not have lasted one week, let alone a year. Instead, I was able to visit remote

Himalayan villages, trek to sacred glacial lakes, paraglide over verdant valleys, catch sight of Kanchenjunga (India's highest peak), study yoga in Southern India, live in an ashram in the Punjab and lounge on Goan beaches.

Patience and discipline go hand in hand. In trapeze I had to develop the discipline to execute the skills and tricks with precision, rather than merely flinging my body around and hoping for the best. Trapeze demanded that I stop rushing. For me, most changes occur in my body first, then in my mind. The action of not rushing helped me develop the mental strength to slow down, breathe and practice patience.

I know now if I want a life that flows with ease and grace, timing is everything.

* * *

## seven

# Don't Quit Before the Miracle

"Let me tell you the secret that has led me to my goal. My strength lies
solely in my tenacity."
— Louis Pasteur

*It's a cool spring day, the fog has lifted, revealing a Riviera blue sky. A lone red-tailed hawk circles slowly above the canopy of dewy oaks; the small stream brought back to life by the recent rain murmurs softly. Standing on the carpeted platform, eye level with the treetops, I reach out to grasp the fly bar. I'm in rarified air for this trapeze class—Tony Steele, one the greatest flying trapeze artists of all time, is visiting the Sonoma trapeze school, offering tips, encouragement and comic relief. At seventy-six, Tony, who is light and agile, still performs a double somersault effortlessly. He offers me advice before I depart the pedestal: "Returning to this board is the only thing that matters."*

*I jump a beat too early. I know my timing is off, but I follow through with the trick—a simple hocks off, which involves hooking my knees on the bar in a straddle position. The instructor and catcher, Marek Kaszuba, somehow catches me, swinging me out over the trapeze apron, and returns me to my own bar. Because my timing is rushed and my trick wonky, I'm low and about to bail without trying to get back up to the pedestal. "Finish the trick!" I hear Tony admonish. I'm dubious, but it's Tony, so I obey, hoisting my legs with great effort, grunting like a weightlifter. I manage to lift my feet just slightly above the board. I release the fly bar and reach for the trapeze upright, sliding onto the platform, landing on my butt. "Good girl," Tony smiles, grabbing me.*

Flying with Tony drummed into me the notion that returning to the platform is the most important aspect of a flying trapeze trick. An ugly trick that results in a return to the board is better than a beautiful trick that doesn't. Tony might not have intended this interpretation, but it was my takeaway from flying with him. Get back on the board no matter what. Finish what I've started.

When learning to return, I'd watched flyers who were far better than I was refuse to come back to the board. They rejected return bars, preferring instead to fall to the net. It can be daunting, after swinging with the catcher and turning in midair, to see the return bar flying straight at your face. The natural, sane reaction is to avoid the bar. But I wasn't burdened with sane reactions in flying trapeze class. Grabbing a return bar came easily to me, which was just about the only aspect of trapeze I picked up quickly. My problem was that my tricks were often mistimed, causing me to lose height and run the risk of being too low to get back on the pedestal. Yet, most of my tricks—as bad as some of them were—ended up back on that platform. Tony's words echoing in my head, coupled with an aversion to falling to the net, helped me develop the gift of tenacity.

My instructors frequently cringed watching me claw my way back onto the board, but tenacity enabled me to stick with the sport that I found fun and rewarding, despite not being a natural at it. Becoming tenacious in trapeze transferred to other areas of my life. By the time I'd taken up trapeze, my career had stalled to the point where many of my regular writing assignments had dried up, victims of magazines going out of business. When I graduated from college in 1988, the Writer's Union suggested freelance writers not accept assignments for less than one dollar a word; by 2005 I was lucky to get thirty cents a word. Yet, new developments in the publishing industry did bode well for writers who were able to weather the demise of print and adjust to new media and new technologies. Tenacity helped me remain committed to my career path, to writing and to evolving with the industry. Tenacity helped me discover ways to economize and streamline. Tenacity saves me from giving up on pursuing what I want and, instead, settling for what I believe I can have. Tenacity helps me expand my definition of what's possible for me.

I've watched many people come into trapeze class and pick it up fairly quickly. I've watched even more show up and progress rather slowly. I've noticed most people from both groups drop out within a year or two. There are always infinite reasons not to pursue something, many of which are legitimate. Quitting because of frustration is not one of them. People who learn quickly will inevitably hit a plateau. Plateaus can last a long time, longer than it took to get to the point of plateau. I've seen people—myself included—stay at virtually the same level for a year. It's frustrating, sure—but progress can't be forced nor can it be willed. We have to try our hardest and give our best effort and then learn to relax and be okay with the process. When people who learn slowly quit, it always seems as if they do so right before they are about to make a breakthrough. Watching them, I can see that they've made small changes that usually lead to a big shift over time.

Sometimes improvements are so small they can't be seen with the naked eye, especially by the person making those improvements. I used to tell myself I was going to quit if I couldn't do such-and-such skill by such-and-such time. That was an absolute setup for failure and for negative motivation. Now I do the opposite. I tell myself I can quit when I learn such-and-such skill. Inevitably when I accomplish that skill, I find I want to set a new goal. Given my inherent limitations as a flying trapeze artist, each new trick I learn, each improvement I make to my swing or takeoff or turnaround, is a bona fide miracle. Every class is an affirmation that I will not quit until I have my next miracle. That is, I will not quit until I am able to do the next thing I think is impossible for me to do.

A miracle can be defined as a shift in perception. When I shift out of thinking something is impossible and shift into thinking of it as a goal, I have already experienced the miracle.

Quitting something because I've found a new passion is a legitimate reason for walking away. Quitting because I've ceased going after the next challenge is not. One of my flying trapeze friends frequently complained that she was bored in class. Bored? How can anyone be bored doing an adventure sport? I'd encourage her to try something new, work on a new trick, a new skill. Wear a new outfit. Develop a new attitude.

For me, quitting trapeze without discovering a new passion or finding a new hobby would be dangerous. I would be susceptible to filling the trapeze void with inertia, lying on my couch, eating chocolates and watching TV or some other non-life-affirming activity. Walking away from trapeze becomes a healthy choice only if I have something healthy lined up to replace it and only if I'm quitting because I'm no longer interested in it. I will not allow myself to quit out of unwillingness to tolerate frustration.

For most of us, success in any area of life requires tenacity: relationships, careers, learning anything new. I used to think if something didn't come to me easily, I wasn't meant to do it; now I know that's not necessarily true. Success is the result of pushing past plateaus, believing in ourselves and committing to seeing our goals through to the end. Success is the result of not quitting before the miracle.

\* \* \*

# *eight*

# Leap of Faith

"There are many talented people who haven't fulfilled their dreams because
they over thought it, or they were too cautious, and were unwilling to
make the leap of faith."
— James Cameron

*Today in class I am experiencing a new level of terror. No longer a brand new
beginner, I'm learning how to move from the absolute novice two-handed takeoff
to the more challenging one-handed takeoff. To accomplish this, I lean out over
the platform with my hips forward and my shoulders pulled back, I reach for
the trapeze bar with my right hand, while my left hand holds onto the upright,
keeping me from being pulled off the platform. I'm now expected to bend my
knees, jump up (as opposed to down, my natural tendency), release the upright
and wait a beat—until my body is in a 7 position in the air—before grabbing
the trapeze bar with my left hand.*

*Leaping up, with only one hand on the bar, trusting that my left hand
will make it there as well, is the most challenging exercise I've faced so far in
trapeze. Every fiber of my being wants to jump down and forward, at the bar
and grab it with my left hand as quickly as possible. Of course, this is precisely
the wrong way to accomplish the takeoff. "No one has ever missed getting their
second hand on the bar," my instructors assure me as I rush to get that left
hand on the bar.*

*I refuse to be soothed. There is always a first time for everything.*

For me, the most difficult moments of flying trapeze occur before I'm actually flying. It's the takeoff—that leap—those moments before I leave the platform, while I'm standing on the edge, that bedevil me most. Once I depart the pedestal, fear becomes displaced by focus. Each time I ready myself for the takeoff, however, I face the same question: am I willing to take this leap of faith, to trust that my second hand will make it to the bar?

Once I'm in the air, a different set of challenges and skills come into play—energy, perseverance, muscle memory, surrender. Before the leap of faith, I have an opportunity to balk and bail and not even bother to try. The leap of faith may be the singular most important action in any endeavor.

For a long, long time, I had a terrible takeoff, which made my leap of faith all the more poignant. Once I was swinging, I could put my crappy takeoff behind me and focus on the trick to come. Trapeze taught me that although it's preferable to be able to execute a good takeoff, it wasn't absolutely necessary for success.

Trapeze taught me how to have faith to start something, despite obstacles to success.

Every beginning requires a leap of faith, a willingness to embrace the unknown. Changing jobs, starting a new relationship, learning a language, taking up a hobby, driving a different route home from work, adopting a dog, deciding to have a child, trying out a new recipe or hairstyle—all actions require a leap of faith.

Some leaps involve a little faith. Some demand a huge amount of faith.

The thousands of leaps I made in trapeze have transferred to other realms of my life. One of my visions for my life was to spend a year traveling. I'd hit a wall with my editorial business, a lousy first draft of a novel and even my location in the ultra-expensive San Francisco Bay Area. I wanted a middle-aged gap year, time to contemplate my next move in life. Choosing to let go of my home, sell or give away most of my possessions and put what I couldn't part with in storage was difficult. It required a tremendous leap of faith. What would I encounter during my travels? What would I return to, and where?

Of course, that year of travel was life-changing and filled with revelations. Except for my first stop—Mysore, India—I traveled without an itinerary, taking leaps of faith along the way. It wasn't always easy. It forced me to stretch and grow in ways even trapeze didn't demand. The result is that I now have friends in every corner of the world, wonderful people I met through my travels. It taught me the beauty of spontaneity.

Landing in my hometown on the East Coast after my travels was another leap of faith. In San Francisco, I enjoyed an abundance of close friendships with likeminded people, a culture that appealed to me, great weather. My hometown is, in some ways, the exact opposite of the Bay Area. I didn't know if I had the skills and drive to start over—new friends, new clients, new activities. Trapeze taught me, however, to focus on one move at a time. It also taught me that there really are endless do-overs in life. If the East Coast doesn't work out, I can return to California or try a new location. I've learned that one wrong step doesn't have to ruin the entire trip.

Today, I have faith that things don't have to go perfectly—or even smoothly—to be successful, and I know I won't go anywhere at all if I don't take that first leap. Every move in life, every change—big and small—starts with a leap of faith.

\* \* \*

*nine*

# Mind Your Eyes, Ears & Mouth

"Concentration is the secret of strength."
— Ralph Waldo Emerson

*Tonight's class is particularly loud. Besides flying trapeze, trampoline, static trapeze and stretching classes are taking place simultaneously in the gym. A professional circus troupe is practicing in the room next to the trapeze rig—each routine accompanied by its own blaring music. A stereo at the foot of the trapeze ladder blasts an endless loop of Gwen Stefani, Fergie and Madonna. Above the din, instructors shout instructions to their students.*

*Standing on the platform, my classmates chat amiably about work, what they had for dinner or where they're going for vacation. I chalk my hands, adjust my outfit, smooth my hair and get ready to fly. I block out everything except the trapeze bar and Hans, who is set to catch my trick. Despite the abundance of activity going on around me, the only person who exists for me right now is Hans.*

Focusing comes easily in trapeze—the sport has a way of creating radical concentration. I'm standing aloft on a platform, listening to the calls of the trapeze catcher who is hanging upside down from a bar on the other side of the rig. When I'm flying, he and I are all that exist. Most tricks take a mere eighteen seconds; sustaining focus for that length of time is no big feat. The real trick is to focus on the right thing at the right time and to take the experience of focusing well for eighteen seconds and expand it to other areas of life.

Although thoughts can cycle so quickly, it may seem as if they're generated simultaneously. Psychologists maintain that our minds can hold only one thought at a time; for this reason, multitasking—a temptation that is hard to resist—never works well for me. If I'm doing two things at once, chances are I'm not doing either of them well.

Multitasking—checking emails, Facebooking, cooking—while on the phone is particularly tempting and futile for me. I can't remember key details of the conversations unless I give the phone calls my full attention. The people to whom I'm speaking deserve my full attention and, though multitasking while talking with them is not meant to be disrespectful, it does diminish our relationship. In one phone conversation during which I multitasked, a friend disclosed that her mom, who had been ill for years, had passed away. Later, I couldn't remember that detail.

Another negative: when I multitask, I tell my subconscious mind that whatever I'm doing isn't important enough to focus on.

Much of my lack of focus is habit. Distractions abound in life on the ground; however, the same is true on the trapeze. Static trapeze classes, which are accompanied by music, as well as trampoline classes are held at the same time as flying trapeze classes; kids run around the gym, the cleaning crew vacuums during morning classes, phones ring, dogs bark loudly outside the gym. Despite all these potential distractions, focusing isn't a problem. Survival instinct seems to aid focus.

I had to work hard to apply the focus that comes easily in trapeze to ordinary life. It requires discipline not to respond to text messages while on a business conference call, to turn off the computer screen while on the phone, to listen to someone else tell the same story for the third time because he or she is too unfocused to remember I've already heard the story. Focus and discipline go hand in hand.

Learning to focus also requires discernment. With so many details affecting every facet of life, choosing the right detail to give attention can be challenging. Much of life's successes are products of choosing details well.

In trapeze, the only details I have to focus on are my execution of the trick and the catcher's instructions. His instructions are generally simple, often just one word: "Hep."

Sometimes, though, he'll give a pep talk before the trick. He'll run down all the things I need to do to be safe and successful. Here's where another key to focus comes into play. The subconscious mind, according to sports psychologists, needs to process information affirmatively. In other words, if the catcher tells me, "Don't rush," my subconscious mind hears, "Rush!"

A better way to instruct is to say, "Patience. Slow down."

In life, as in trapeze, we can't control the way others communicate. We can, however, control what we hear. Each time my catcher says, "Don't rush," I counter with my own silent affirmation, "Patience," or "My timing is perfect." What I tell myself is always more powerful than anything anyone else tells me.

What we focus on grows. If I focus on the negatives, I will create and perpetuate negative feelings and experiences. If I focus my attention on positives, I create more goodness. I learned to accentuate the positive to overcome, or at least compensate for, the negative.

When my trapeze takeoff was lousy and I kept focusing on how poorly I performed it, I made no improvements. When I started focusing on what I did well or how I could compensate for a poor takeoff, my trapeze experience began improving.

Focus and concentration need to be embraced holistically. Everything starts with a thought. Thoughts produce feelings and feelings drive actions. Therefore, if I have a negative thought—"my takeoff stinks," for example—I will create anxiety. Anxiety causes me to rush, grab the bar early, fight momentum to get into position, release the bar early and hurl myself into the catcher. That one negative thought just set off an avalanche of negativity. Such is the power of thought.

Trapeze crystallized the power of thoughts for me. Negative thoughts create negative energy, and it's much more difficult to fly free if my energy is pulling me down.

One sure way to create positive focus and energy is to start and end the day with a gratitude list. Since what we focus on grows, if we're constantly looking for things to add to the gratitude list, we will find an inexhaustible supply.

Knowing that you get what you focus on is the first step to creating the life you want. Make sure your eyes, ears and mouth focus on the positive.

* * *

*ten*

# People Who Need People

"If everyone helps to hold up the sky, then one person does not become tired."
– Askhari Johnson Hodari (*Lifelines: The Black Book of Proverbs*)

*I've reached the level I've simultaneously looked forward to and dreaded since I began flying trapeze classes: it's time for me to try returning my tricks to the platform, the final piece of a trapeze performance. Painstaking work has gone into reaching this point. I've developed my swing to create enough height for successful returns. Several of my beginner tricks are solid enough for returns. I've learned to trust myself and my instructors. Now is the moment to put it all together and take my trust to a new level. A triumphant return to platform requires a well-timed return bar, which I must receive from one of my fellow fly-ers. Tonight I'll learn to rely on my classmates to help me succeed.*

*My trick—a half-turn to Hans, which gives me a chance to practice the half-turn I will need to do to grab my return bar—is smooth and steady. My timing is dead on. I make the catch, swing with Hans, ride our swing to the top of the trapeze arc, push off him, turn and see the trapeze bar zooming straight at my face. I freeze for a nanosecond, unsure of what to do. Then, I grab the bar, sweep my legs behind me, drive them forward, release the bar and reach for the trapeze rig upright. I land back on the platform to a rousing applause from my classmates, instructors and others who happen to be in the gym. I'm elated, but I know I can't take credit for this huge accomplishment. Hans is an amazing catcher and much of the credit for my trapeze success goes to him. As importantly, Shannon dropped me the perfect return bar. Without the witnesses—everyone else in the gym pulling for me—my accomplishment would not have tasted as sweet to me.*

No flying trapeze trick is a solo performance. Although flying trapeze usually highlights one flyer at a time, the sport is, in my opinion, the ultimate team sport. From beginner level through the most difficult trick (the quadruple somersault) all trapeze activities are a group effort. Beginners rely on instructors pulling their safety lines, helping with their takeoffs and calling out directions on what to do. Flyers at every level rely on the catcher to catch the trick—even when it's not quite perfectly timed—and safely return them to their own trapeze bars.

Flyers work together in service to each other. We take risers in and out for each other and hand each other the fly bar. We help prepare the person whose turn it is to fly. Once the flyer makes the catch—that is, swings out, performs the trick and is caught by the catcher—we drop the flyer's bar for her return to the platform. We also help scoop her back up to the platform when necessary. Dropping the return bar, a skill no one even notices when watching a flying trapeze performance, is one of the most important things we do for each other.

Dropping a return bar is part timing, part intuition and part luck. Luck, timing and intuition increase with familiarity and caring. In trapeze, community is essential, since community builds intimacy and fosters understanding.

As the least accomplished flyer in my trapeze group, being a good teammate became a particular source of pride for me. In the early days of my flying with the advanced flyers, I had a habit of sucking all the attention out of the gym. My neediness and fear demanded that the instructors constantly coddle me. I can imagine this grew grating—and old—quickly for my classmates. As my self-centered fear began to diminish, I was able to give back to, rather than constantly take from, trapeze class. One way I could give back, long before I became a competent flyer, was to become proficient at dropping return bars for other flyers. I became a good teammate before I became a good soloist. Being a good teammate contributed significantly to my flying skills.

I developed the skill of dropping return bars by watching the other flyers closely, paying attention to their height and timing. The more attention I paid them, the less I paid myself and the happier I became. Trapeze helped me discover a key to happiness: not thinking about myself.

By focusing on others, all of my negative character traits eased up to some degree. My flying improved. Focusing on others helped me develop some of my deepest friendships with people I admire, respect and aspire to emulate. Most importantly, becoming focused on others and creating community increased my self-esteem. I began to feel like a part of a pack; I began to feel useful. Community gave me strength, courage and tons of fun.

My trapeze experience taught me well. As a frequent traveler, I know how to find community wherever I go. In Kashmir, India, I met up with other skiers. In Mysore, India, other yogis. In Ubud, Bali, I volunteered at an animal rescue. Volunteering always brings close friendships. During long-term stays in one destination, I join the local library, show up at the same café every day and get to know the other regulars and accept invitations to do things, even when doing so is extremely uncomfortable.

As a freelance writer, I can't rely on a job to help me create community. Phone calls, Facebook and text messages do not a community make. Out of necessity, I've learned to seek out likeminded people and join the groups to which they belong. This skill is among the most important I've learned. I've relocated numerous times, moving back and forth across the country. Community has eased every transition and made me feel at home.

When Laura moved from Portland, Oregon, to a small town in Northeast Pennsylvania, within days she'd found several communities. She joined a church—as a diehard adherent to a peripatetic lifestyle, Laura says the individual congregation matters far more to her than the doctrine to which they ascribe. She also started taking aerial silks classes, which is how we met. Like always attracts like.

People are pack animals. Even the most introverted among us needs to belong to a group. The support and sustenance from being a part of something bigger than oneself brings blessings, joy, challenges, opportunities for growth and the necessity of letting go of selfish interests. Relief from thinking about myself, I've found, brings me bliss. This is only possible through community. People need people.

\* \* \*

*eleven*

# If You Want to Fly, Prepare to Fall

"The most important thing in life is learning how to fall."
— Jeannette Walls (*Half Broke Horses*)

*I'm warming up on the trapeze, practicing my splits position on the bar and then pulling myself out of it, and backdropping to the net. I enjoy backdropping. It's the only time I feel utterly relaxed in the air while holding on to neither the trapeze bar nor the catcher. To perform the backdrop, I wait until I'm at the top of my swing, completely motionless. Then I push the bar hard away from me, look up the ceiling, squeeze my legs and butt and float to the net, landing on my back. I love this sensation.*

*Today, though, the instructors are insisting I take my net skills to the next level. Instead of pulling myself out of the splits position and backdropping to the net, I must release the bar while still in the splits, sweep my front leg behind me, fall face first toward the net and, at the last moment, half-turn so that I land on my back.*

Falling to the net is a basic skill every trapeze student learns. Rule number one in flying trapeze: the flyer must always land on her back when she falls to the net. This is only way to ensure we are safe. Landing on our backs protects our limbs and face and also allows us to bounce and perform net tricks—somersaults, for example. Flyers spend hours practicing how to land on our backs, a counter-instinctual move. When we're falling, our natural impulse is to put our hands out in front of us and try to break our fall. We tend to look in the direction we're falling. In trapeze, looking where you're falling means looking at the net; and if you're looking at the net, you're headed for it face first—a totally natural response and an excellent way to get hurt.

In trapeze, the most important skill for ensuring safety is knowing how to fall. Falling is not only inevitable, it's often preferable—and safer—than completing a wonky or badly-timed trick. Falling, in trapeze, is not necessarily a mistake. Often, it's a choice.

For a long time when I was practicing falling, I felt like Wile E. Coyote barreling off a cliff while chasing the roadrunner. I'd hear my instructor shout, "Turn!" and I so wanted to be able to comply by completing that half-turn to my back, but I would not take my eyes off the net. I'd fling my hands out in front of my face. My instructor would bail me out by tightening up my safety lines and breaking my fall.

Like most of my trapeze misadventures, this went on for much longer than is reasonable. Finally, I got it: if I want to spend the rest of my trapeze time wearing safety lines, learning to fall isn't an issue. If, however, I want to fly free, I first have to be willing to fall. Flying well would never determine my safety in trapeze. Falling well would.

In everyday life, falling is usually associated with failure. The bigger the goal, the greater the risk of falling. Fear of falling—fear of failure—can hold me back in so many areas of life. Fear of falling has a tendency to grow exponentially with every fall. One failed relationship makes each successive relationship increasingly difficult to initiate. In my professional life, every editorial rejection hangs over all subsequent projects.

In life, as in trapeze, I always have a safety net. My safety net here in the real world is comprised of community, books and stories by authors sharing their paths to greater freedom and joy; meditation, yoga and other spiritual practices that help me feel safe and supported.

While I still feel tremendous disappointment each time I fall, I no longer spend most of my time looking for the safety net. I know it's always there. I know now it's safe—even fun—to fall.

\* \* \*

*twelve*

# Between the Bars

"Holding on is believing there's only a past; letting go is knowing
that there's a future."
— Daphne Rose Kingma

*I release my splits to the net. Even without the benefit of mirrors, I know
exactly what I look like—a bug that's just been dropped on its back in water:
frenzied, kicking wildly, desperately. After hundreds of trapeze classes, I've
become almost comfortable with swinging, catching, even returning to the
platform. As long as I'm holding onto something or about to grab something,
I'm good. Here, in midair, however, without a bar or catcher in sight, my fear
resurfaces. I loathe this feeling of being in between where I am and where I'm
going.*

There is a moment in virtually every trapeze trick when the flyer
has let go of the bar but has not yet been caught by the catcher. There
is also a moment when the flyer, after being released by the catcher,
has not yet grabbed the return bar. Most successful trapeze tricks reach
two points when the flyer is between the bars.

Between the bars are moments of true flight. Between the bars
are moments of true freedom. When I first started trapeze, between

the bars were moments of true terror. Now, between the bars are opportunities to assess my situation and—through a combination of skill, intuition, and experience—choose my next right move. Even the act of not making a choice is really a choice. The one action I know I can't choose is to head back in the direction from which I came. My choices are either continuing on with forward momentum or falling.

When we're between the bars, there's no going back. We can decide not to move forward—we can pull our hands back and not make the catch or refuse to finish the trick—but we can't go back to the beginning and start over.

For most trapeze tricks, the flyer releases the bar without seeing the catcher, without knowing if the timing is right for a catch or if she'll miss and fall to the net. The same is usually true of the return bar. Being between the bars is really a moment of faith. We have to trust that the catcher or the bar will be where they're supposed to be or, if they're not, we must have confidence in our own skills of falling safely to the net.

Life's transitional periods are times when we're between the bars. A relationship has ended, and often it's impossible to imagine ever trusting or loving again. A career path has reached a dead end and we have no idea how to reapply our skills. Or, we lack enthusiasm for our lives, or look to our partners or children to infuse our lives with meaning, only to realize we can't rely on others to define us. We're left feeling as if we've lost our identity.

When we're between the bars in life, those transition periods can feel endless, hopeless and dark. Between the bars can be much easier to handle if we're prepared, if we know how to fall and if our safety net is in place. Being able to rely on the strength, experience and hope provided by community helps ease the discomfort of those moments when you are between the life you had and the life you're heading towards.

* * *

# *thirteen*

# Go Big or Stay Home

"Our deepest fear is not that we are inadequate. Our deepest fear is that we are powerful beyond measure. It is our Light, not our Darkness, that most frightens us."
— Marianne Williamson

*Standing on the platform, holding the trapeze bar, Cory wears a fuchsia leotard and black boy shorts that emphasize her long, lean legs. Her bare toes, which will be pointed from the moment she leaves the platform until she returns to it, are painted to match her outfit. Beside her on the board, two women also dressed to fly assist Cory. One removes the riser after Cory's takeoff; the other watches Cory closely to determine how high to send her the return bar. Both stand ready to scoop Cory back onto the platform, if needed. While Cory gets into her trick position, the catcher gauges her swing and adjusts his own so that they can make a perfect catch. On the ground, the other instructor studies Cory, ready to coach her if she needs help. The rest of the class—and everyone who happens to be in the gym—is watching Cory as well.*

*This is Cory's moment in the spotlight.*

Like many of us, Cory both craves and dreads the attention. Shining in the limelight can be intimidating or embarrassing or may evoke feelings of being undeserving of the attention. Cory says she considers herself a behind-the-scenes person, not a performer, but she knows she needs attention to succeed in trapeze. Shunning attention in trapeze class would be counterproductive; no one can develop new skills without the benefit of others' attention. The ability to perform despite scrutiny demands focus and confidence. To progress in trapeze—and to enjoy the process—Cory, like many of us, had to learn to step out of the background and stand, front and center, in the spotlight.

Putting yourself, your work or your art out for all to see is not easy for most people. A range of insecurities can surface—awkwardness, shame, feelings of not being good enough and even pride and arrogance. I see people who fail to step into the spotlight professionally because they feel entitled to success without having to market themselves or sell their services. They believe the good should come their way, without their seeking it. This might work for a lucky minority. Most of us, however, have to sell the hell out of ourselves to succeed. We have to grab the brass ring.

For a trapeze trick to be safe and successful, the flyer needs everyone to focus on her. She needs the instructor to call out the timing of the trick; if his attention is elsewhere, the flyer must ask for it to be turned to her. If the other students are chatting and distracting the flyer, she has to be able to ask them to be quiet and let her focus. If the flyer can't bring herself to ask for everyone's attention, she is putting her safety in peril and depriving herself of a full flying experience.

In life, if we can't ask for the attention we need to be happy, healthy and successful, whether through interpersonal relationships or mass marketing our goods and services, we are unlikely to meet our personal and professional goals.

Being the focus of attention sometimes seems selfish, especially for those who are taught to put everyone before themselves. Learning how to ask for attention, however, can teach us how to be better at giving it. One of the flyers in our gym is notoriously demanding when it's her turn to fly. She dictates a long list of extremely precise instructions for the person assisting her, such as how to serve her the bar, how to put up and take down her riser and how to send her return bar. I used to dread assisting her—until one day when she assisted me. On the platform, she asked how she could help make my trapeze experience more fun and successful. She listened carefully to my list of instructions. While I was in the spotlight, she gave me her full focus and sent me a perfect return bar. I realized then that her requests for our attention had not been selfish; she wasn't being difficult. She was just clear about what she needed to complete her performance—which translated into a great ability to give others what they needed.

Once we realize there are times when it is appropriate and necessary to ask for attention and begin to let go of our inhibitions, we usually find ourselves enjoying the spotlight. When we accomplish—or attempt—something profound, it's important to have acknowledgement. We need and deserve it. When I'm claiming the spotlight in trapeze class, I'm saying, "Look at me because I need your assistance," and I'm also saying, "Look at me because what I'm about to do is astonishing to me and I need you to witness it." Learning to enjoy attention is one way of honoring the work you've done to earn it, which in turn builds self-esteem.

Once we surrender to our human need for validation and accept the goodness that comes our way, we find it easier to give attention to others.

Enjoying our spotlight also means not being distracted by what's going on in other people's lives. We deserve to have our time in the spotlight, our shot at success, even if those close to us are not experiencing a comparable level of fulfillment. Many people are hesitant to allow themselves to become more successful than their parents, partners or siblings. As we attain goals greater than those our loved ones achieved, or create richer lives than they did, we can start to feel guilty and sabotage our own success. It's difficult to shine when the people we love are not; but to paraphrase Nelson Mandela, our "playing small" so that others don't have to feel threatened by us does not serve. It doesn't help them and it devastates us. Without recognition we develop a deprivation mentality and become starved for attention, which can lead to chronic feelings of being ignored or slighted. It can cause anger and resentment, which sets off a cascade of negative consequences on every level—physical, mental, emotional and spiritual.

Playing small, or holding back, has another negative consequence in trapeze: not giving a trapeze trick everything I have to give makes me more vulnerable to injury. When I play small in trapeze and squirm in the spotlight, that holding back tends to filter into my tricks. I'll do the trick halfheartedly. Sometimes my insecurity or embarrassment about grabbing the attention will tell tales, making me believe playing small keeps me safe physically, because I'm not moving as fast or with as much force. Playing small, I mistakenly believe, will keep me safe emotionally because I'll avoid the scrutiny from instructors and classmates.

Holding back—playing small—keeps my swing low, which keeps my body low when I release the trick to the catcher. When I'm playing small, my inner voice tells me that height is scary and unsafe; it tells me to stay close to the net because the net is my only friend. Ironically, the opposite is true. In trapeze, height is my friend. The higher I am, the further away from the net I am and the more time I have to react and get my body into a safe position for landing in the net, if necessary.

We all tend to find what we're looking for; we draw to us what we spend the most mental and emotional energy on. When we let fear get the better of us, we cause what we had hoped to avoid. For instance, fear of rejection can keep us from initiating a friendship with someone we find attractive and interesting. We begin to believe lies, keeping our lives small in the mistaken belief that small equals safe. We avoid risks for fear of getting hurt. But if we won't take the risk, we obliterate the possibility of getting what we want. We live in fearful reaction to what comes our way, rather than grabbing the spotlight and going after what we truly want.

This is what I've learned from life on the flying trapeze (and in the net): not going for what I want, with all of my focus and energy, ensures that I will not get what I want. I won't accomplish the goals I set outside trapeze. I won't have the job, relationship, home or quality of life I want. I won't risk the discomfort of solo travel and I'll miss out on all the magical encounters that could only happen because I took that risk.

I know that playing small will get me small results. Giving any endeavor everything I have to give, on the other hand, imbues me with a sense of vitality and accomplishment, even when the endeavor doesn't work out as I'd hoped. While I've regretted holding back and not doing all I could to fulfill a goal, I've never once regretted striving for a goal with all my might. I've learned to embrace the spotlight.

\* \* \*

# fourteen
# Make a New Mistake

"You wanna fly, you got to give up the shit that weighs you down."
— Toni Morrison (*Song of Solomon*)

*Scene: Four flying trapeze hobbyists, friends who spend several hours a week trapezing together, are on the rig looking glum and stressed. The irony being, of course, trapeze is what these four middle-aged women do for fun. One climbs the ladder after a clunky fall to the net. Another violently chalks her hands, covering herself with chalk residue. A third swings the trapeze bar back and forth to herself, muttering under her breath. The fourth flyer argues with her instructor on the ground. One by one, they take turns flying, each working on a different skill. One by one, turn after turn, their frustration escalates as they each make the same mistakes over and over.*

*Forty-five minutes pass. Finally, one flyer, Teresa, says, "I've had it. This time I'm going to do something different. Even if I screw up, at least I'll make a new mistake."*

*Off Teresa flies. True to her word, she tries something different. It works! The trick is a success for the first time that class. By that point, Teresa said later, she'd given up on doing the trick correctly. She just wanted to stop doing the thing she knew would not work. By then, she understood the futility—and insanity—of doing the same thing over and over and expecting a different result.*

Mistakes in trapeze can be tricky. Because there is an element of danger in trapeze, anything that doesn't result in injury can, on some level, be considered successful. Making changes in trapeze entails venturing into the unknown. When I repeatedly make the same mistake, I experience a false sense of control. By doing the same thing, albeit incorrectly, at least I know what the result will be. Changing my behavior means I'll get a new, unknown, result. I have to face my fear of the unknown.

Sometimes making the same mistake over and over has nothing to do with fear. It's just muscle memory or habit. Breaking bad habits can be even more challenging than facing fear of the unknown.

It takes twenty-one days to break a habit or to establish a new habit. It also takes consciousness and courage, as well as healthy eating and plenty of sleep. I've noticed my natural predisposition to being short-tempered and impatient is much easier to curb when I'm not hungry or tired.

The solution and the problem are never the same thing. I can't experience a change in my circumstances until I'm willing to change my behavior. The great news is that I don't have to wait until I want to change my behavior. I don't have to wait for my feelings to shift before I make a change. I just have to take action and continue with the new action until my feelings catch up.

In trapeze, when I initially became willing to stop rushing, my timing slowed down so much that, for several weeks, I was always a beat too slow. The result was still a botched trick, but at least it was a different kind of mistake. Eventually, I found the sweet spot with my timing. Being willing to stop rushing enabled me to correct my timing.

In life, when I make changes to my behavior, I may not get it right the first time I try something new. I've found that willingness to let go of what doesn't work opens up infinite possibilities for something that *does* work to happen. All it takes is willingness to change, and willingness to change sometimes starts with making a new mistake.

* * *

# *fifteen*
# What's the Worst That Could Happen?

"Have no fear of perfection—you'll never reach it."
— Salvador Dalí

*I'm sitting on a wooden bench in the gym, a safety belt snugly pulled around my waist, watching my classmates fly. I'm the only one in the class still wearing a safety belt for the entire class. Everyone else swings without safety lines and performs at least one trick without them. Some perform advanced tricks without lines. Watching my classmates fly, I feel overwhelmed with admiration and, much to my dismay, envy. It's not the fact that they can fly without lines, nor their beautiful tricks, that incites my jealousy. It's their demeanors, the look on their faces—every one of them seems completely relaxed—I find most impressive. They look as if they don't even realize they are twenty feet—or thirty feet, or more—in the air. From my perspective, they are the exact opposite of me—they are confident, bold, fearless.*

After thirteen years of psychotherapy, I discovered many things about myself. I even managed to make some significant emotional and behavioral changes. What didn't change, however, were my fears. Fear of failure, fear of success, fear of love, fear of people, fear of being abandoned, fear of being consumed, fear of consuming too much and more, including fear of heights. A universe of self-help and New Age slogans swirl through my mind when I ponder fear. Fear is the opposite of faith. Fear is an acronym: false evidence appearing real. All troublesome character traits are a manifestation of fear. Greed and gluttony: fear there won't be enough for me. Envy: fear that other peoples' successes somehow preclude me from attaining my own. Dishonesty: fear that I'm not good enough. Anger and resentment: fear that someone has taken, or will take, what's mine. On the flip side, love is letting go of fear.

Thirteen years of psychotherapy and over twenty-two years of recovery from compulsive, self-destructive behaviors gave me wads of self-knowledge. I know *why* I'm fearful. Unfortunately, I haven't found knowing *why* to be particularly helpful in overcoming, or befriending, fear.

Trapeze gave me a question I find more valuable when facing fear. Now when fear struts into my psyche, I ask myself: what's the worst that could happen?

The one trapeze trick I wanted to nail more than any other is the splits. Generally performed by women only, the splits position shows off my best asset on the trapeze: flexibility.

To perform the splits, the flyer leaves the platform, performs a swing by sweeping her legs behind her and driving her legs and hips forward, building height. She straightens out her body, pikes her legs slightly, sweeps both legs behind her and floats her legs up. One leg goes straight up against the bar and the other leg bends and straightens out under the bar, so that the flyer is upside down in a split with her back arched, facing the catcher. This book's cover features me in a splits position.

At the release to the catcher, the flyer simply extends her arms forward. As a beginner trick, a splits position on the bar doesn't involve spinning or twisting or anything truly skillful. Yet, it was the trick that scared me the most. Every time I was ready to perform the splits—and I performed the splits several times every class, two or three classes a week, for four years—my fear ratcheted up.

It made no sense. The splits is my best trick. The splits is the trick I practice all the time. I even had a practice trapeze bar installed in my apartment, just so I could practice the splits position at home. How could I fear doing something I do all the time?

After standing on the platform for the thousandth time, compulsively chalking my hands as if the action of chalking up would alleviate my fear, worrying I wouldn't perform my splits correctly, I looked down at the net and over at the other students on the ground, all of whom were performing far more difficult, dangerous tricks than I was. My mind was beginning its usual "why, why, why I am so scared," when I finally stopped and asked myself, what's the worst that could happen?

I took a few deep breaths and tried to imagine a disastrous result with the splits. I couldn't. For a simple trick like the splits, the worst that could happen would be that I fail to get into the position correctly. Since I'm strong enough to hold onto the bar even when I screw up, falling to the net wasn't a legitimate concern. The worst thing that could happen was that I wouldn't achieve my desired result with the trick.

When I considered this, I realized I wasn't afraid of getting hurt. I wasn't afraid of falling. I was afraid of *failing*. I was afraid to do a trick I do well, simply because I was afraid I wouldn't do it well.

The worst that could happen is that I would be embarrassed. The worst that could happen is that I would not be perfect.

For much of my life, perfectionism has held me back. I'd always viewed my perfectionism as laudable. I want everything to be perfect; what could possibly be wrong with that? Plenty, it turns out.

Months after I'd been performing those splits without safety lines, a more advanced flyer, Teresa, was watching my class. I told her my goal for that night was to catch the splits without safety lines. Modest goal, but of course, I was scared. Teresa told me she was going to stay for my whole class and support me in this goal. She told me that all I had to do was swing into splits position on the bar. She said I didn't have to do the perfect splits position and I didn't have to release the trick. All I had to do, she said, was try to get into position because I would feel better for having tried. I was dubious. All my protestations came up. "What if can't get into position? What if I can't hold the position? What if I bend my front leg? What if I look bad?" "Doesn't matter," she said, "just try."

Since she waited an hour and a half just to watch me try, I felt obligated to do what she said. I got into splits position, held the position and released for a successful catch. It was not my most beautiful splits. It was not a beautiful catch. But I did it. And I tell you what: Teresa was right. I felt great.

Perfectionism potentially dampens every facet of life. Perfectionism is not a character attribute, a fine quality that makes me a better person. Perfectionism is a curse that ruins projects, relationships, travels, creativity. Perfectionism searches for what's wrong, not what's right, in every situation. Perfectionism demands complete submission. Perfectionism hates fun: strolling on sandy beaches, stomping in warm springtime puddles, anything that isn't one hundred percent tidy. Perfectionism feeds and breeds fear.

Shortly after my watershed moment with Teresa, I was in class and had performed a splits, catch and return, meaning I swung into the splits position, had been caught by the catcher, swung with him, returned to my own bar and then stepped back up on the pedestal. Since returning to the pedestal is the goal of every trick, I was pleased with myself. Back on ground, one of my instructors was watching a DVR replay of the trick in slow motion, pointing out all the things I could have done better. He had a lot of material to work with. As I listened to him, I felt my euphoric mood begin to crash. Of course, I want to perform to the best of my ability, but that is precisely what I'd done. I watched the video while he complained about how my trick looked. I asked him for the remote and turned off the DVR. I turned to him. "You're crazy," I said. "I'm beautiful."

I was not about to let *his* perfectionism ruin my trapeze high.

Perfectionism is a bigger gremlin in the attainment of joy than fear, because perfectionism masquerades as something noble. Perfectionism must not be befriended. It must be obliterated. In reality, perfectionism looks, feels, tastes, smells and sounds a lot like fear. It even produces one of the same responses that fear does: freeze (deer in the headlights), fight (rattlesnake in the grass about to be trod upon) and flight (flying trapeze artist feeling the fear and doing it anyway).

Putting this book out there is my greatest exercise in relinquishing perfectionism. There are so many other elements I wanted to include, but I'd never finish. I knew I could find endless reasons to continue writing and never publish this book. I knew it would never be perfect. I also know that perfect is an illusion.

Fear is not the enemy. The enemy is perfectionism. Not going for what we want in life is *the* worst thing that could happen.

\* \* \*

*sixteen*

# Visualize the Result You Want

"Everything you can imagine is real."
— Pablo Picasso

*Advanced trapeze class: we are all working on returning to the platform. Like every other sport, trapeze is ninety-five percent mental; at this stage of the game, as practiced as we all are, the other five percent is...mental.*

*One of the flyers has just accepted a return bar she should have refused. Had she been flying with more awareness, after her half-turn to face the return bar and platform, she would have ignored the return bar, performed a second half-turn and fallen to the net, landing on her back. Instead, she grabbed a badly-timed return bar that was too low for her. Her forearms smacked down onto the bar with a loud whack. Valiantly, she continued, trying to finish her trick by landing back on the platform. Instead, she peeled off the bar at the worst possible moment and fell hard to the net, landing on her head. A collective gasp escaped everyone else in the gym, as the instructors jumped up into the net to assist her.*

*I'm the next flyer up. The image of what just happened cycles through my head. "That could be me," I think. "I'm self-employed; I can't afford to be injured." I frequently perform lousy returns and exhibit bad judgment—grabbing hold of return bars I have no business accepting. For me, instinct takes over when I'm going for the catch or returning to the platform. I see something to grab hold of and, regardless of whether it's a good idea or not, I instinctively go for it. Right now, I can't shake the image of what just happened to the flyer before me, but I know I must. I take a few deep breaths, close my eyes and change my mental pictures. I see the flyer before me and then myself as I would like us to be—returning safely to the platform.*

For trapezists flying at about twenty-five miles per hour while performing multiple skills during an eighteen-second span, time is not on our side. As a slow learner, one of the most daunting aspects of flying trapeze for me is the fact that everything on the trapeze happens so fast. Unlike dance and other physical activities in which I've participated, skills can't be broken down, demonstrated or practiced slowly on the flying trapeze. Conversely, tricks can't be repeated quickly, since learning something new involves climbing the ladder, fastening into safety lines, preparing for takeoff, trying out the trick, landing in the net and climbing the ladder again to start the process all over. Trapeze tricks are short; but the time in between each turn to practice them is long.

Visualization, I learned, is key in flying trapeze. I couldn't learn how to do anything beyond the most basic beginner level until I first could see myself doing it in my imagination. Trapeze drove home the notion for me that form follows thought.

When learning a new trick, or seeking to improve an established trick, it's helpful to watch videos of someone accomplished performing the skill in slow motion. I am not an intuitive learner. To understand movements, I need to analyze them. Understanding what I need to do and actually doing it, are quite different. Bogging myself down in the minutiae of every trick can kill the spirit of flying free. Once I know what I want my body to do, I need to focus on the result I'm trying to achieve before stepping off the platform. I need to visualize. If I've done my homework and am prepared to perform the skill, I need to trust my training and not overwhelm myself with details. When it's time to perform, before stepping off the board, I see myself wrist-to-wrist with the catcher and then I see myself stepping back up onto the pedestal. I let the details take care of themselves.

I began applying this philosophy to the rest of my life. Instead of trying to imagine how every element of a goal—traveling, relocating, publishing a book—would play out, I began focusing on the result I want to achieve. Of course, there are always numerous actions I have to take to bring an aspiration to fruition. Focusing on the result doesn't mean I get to avoid taking all the necessary steps and it doesn't mean I don't enjoy the process. Focusing on the result gives providence a chance to act in my life. It helps me surrender the impulse to control every detail.

Wrangling every detail of any undertaking is one sure way to destroy spontaneity, flow and joy. It might even destroy success. Visualizing the result helps clarify goals, needs and desires, and it allows for intuition and inspiration to work magic in my life.

Now that I visualize the results of each goal—whether they're on the trapeze, in my career or elsewhere—one of two things happens. Either the necessary steps to achieving the goal are revealed to me through inspiration or coincidence; or I lose interest in the goal. Visualization gives me clarity about where I want to be in every area of my life.

To make visualization work for you, practice seeing and feeling as if you've attained the situation or condition you desire. If, for example, you wish to be in an intimate relationship, focus on seeing yourself happily coupled; imagine what it would feel like to give and receive love, support, comfort, joy and understanding. Avoid imagining your-self with a specific person, but rather focus on the feelings you would like to share in your ideal relationship. The goal of visualization is to see yourself as you would like to be, not to try to control others.

Ultimately, happiness is the goal of all other goals. Holding an image of yourself as happy, without trying to direct every detail of your path, allows options to open up that you might not have considered.

* * *

*seventeen*

# Rainbow Feelings

"Feelings come and go like clouds in a windy sky..."
— Thich Nhat Hanh

*"You're still afraid of heights?" An acquaintance asks, incredulous, after watching a video of me on the trapeze. "Why would you keep doing something that scares you?"*

The answer is obvious to me: because it's fun. Trapeze *is* scary, but it's also exhilarating and fun and amusing and frustrating and rewarding and illuminating. Often I feel all of these emotions at the same time. Trapeze has helped me learn to hold seemingly contradictory feelings simultaneously.

Before trapeze, I'd long known of my tendency towards black and white thinking. Going through life constantly labeling people, places, things and events as good or bad, right or wrong, perpetuated my lack of emotional maturity. If things were going the way I wanted them to go, I labeled that good. When I didn't get my way, it was bad. I remember, years ago, a friend commenting on my black and white thinking. What she said has stuck with me: It's the colors in life that are beautiful.

Trapeze is a colorful activity. A trick can fail miserably and still be fun. Falling to the net can be fun. Learning anything new always involves a learning curve, which makes each new skill acquired a potentially frustrating experience. It's up to me to choose to view the process as fun and rewarding, despite frustration. Even during my most terrifying moments in trapeze someone may say something that makes me laugh out loud. No trapeze experience stirs up only one emotion.

Such is true of real life. Even during some of my darkest moments—mourning the loss of my sister and father, for example—there are always rays of light. Serenity and profound sorrow can coexist.

Most intimate relationships involve navigating the wide spectrum of emotions that intimacy triggers. Knowing I can feel anger and love simultaneously has helped assuage the anxiety that accompanies rough patches in my closest relationships. Now, instead of being whipped around by my emotions, I have the presence to feel them and let them pass. No feeling lasts forever. No feeling exists without myriad emotional responses. I'm learning to embrace all the colors of my emotions.

\* \* \*

# eighteen
## Dressing the Part

"One should either be a work of art, or wear a work of art."
– Oscar Wilde

*High above the platform, standing on a riser, a huge grin stretches across my face as I wait for the catcher to call me off the board. I'm wearing one of my favorite outfits—teal Brazilian yoga pants, with golden Shivas silkscreened on each calf, a gauzy short ballet skirt in blue-hued watercolors over the pants, a carnelian orange tank topping off the costume. I feel excited, eager, in joyful anticipation of a successful trapeze trick—a layout, which is a somersault in a straight body position. My confidence has been buoyed by a seeming jump, after a long plateau, in my trapeze proficiency—at least that's what the logical part of my brain thinks. I have to admit, though, that I started feeling more poised when I overheard my trapeze instructor, Paris, point to me, and say to another student, "Look at what she's wearing. She's very stylish." As I reach for the trapeze bar, Paris calls up to me, "You're the best-dressed flyer in the gym today."*

While I know I possess at least average vanity, I've never been a glamour girl. I don't care much about clothes or makeup or accessories, or externals of any kind. I'm all about feelings. I choose comfort over appearance nearly one hundred percent of the time. It just so happens that trapeze clothes—leotards, tights, yoga pants, Lycra shorts, camisoles with shelf bras, leg warmers—are comfortable.

Trapeze is one arena where I'm able to combine total comfort with color and style.

When I first took up flying trapeze, during one of the Bay Area's wettest winters, the gym in which I began flying was frequently damp and always cold. I would pile on layers of worn sweatshirts over old tights and sweatpants. I looked dumpy, felt dumpy and flew dumpy. After a few weeks, I realized my outfits were not only not helping me, they were hurting me. I felt heavy and unattractive, which is the exact opposite of the sensations I was going for. I reminded myself of the snowsuit-bundled kid brother in the movie *A Christmas Story*. I was in desperate need of a new trapeze wardrobe—something warm and comfortable, yet attractive and light. I began wearing close-fitted cashmere sweaters over my leotards, knit tights, leg warmers that complemented my sweater and cashmere socks. The results were immediate: I felt better. I flew better. I learned that it's easier to feel good if I believe I look good. Feeling good translated directly into better performances.

I also came to realize that my choices in dressing were one of the few things about trapeze—and life—that I could control. How I felt, the outcome of the trick and even my own progression, were all beyond my ability to control. My outfit was not. I began dressing according to my feelings and my goals. On trapeze days when I feel bold and I want to tackle a new challenge, I dress in flashy, bright-colored outfits that highlight my muscles and make me feel powerful. On days when I want to focus on the catch, I choose a lacy, lower-cut top, black fishnets and tiny shorts, imagining the catcher will work harder to get me if I seem sexy and desirable. On days when my energy flags and my goal is a more mellow trapeze experience, I go understated, choosing pieces that call no unwanted attention to me. I use my outfits to help me communicate and convey how I wish to be treated, both to myself and others.

Living in the Bay Area—where every day is casual Friday—for many years as a freelance writer, I'd forgotten how to dress for success. I thought back to my first job out of college, in New York City. The editor told me he'd whittled the candidates down to two; the curve-hugging, cleavage-highlighting, confidence-boosting suit I wore for the second interview broke the tie. (This was back in the Eighties; I can't imagine anyone being foolish enough to make that sort of statement today.) Back then, I felt insulted, but I took away the lesson. During the ensuing twenty years since that interview, I'd forgotten about the power of looking good.

Consciously or unconsciously, how we dress sends out strong messages. People treat us differently depending on our appearance.

We also treat ourselves differently. When we take care to choose clothing that reflects who we are at any given moment, we send the same message to ourselves that we are sending out into the world. Regardless of how we feel—whether bold, strong, sexy or demure—looking good helps us feel good. Feeling good works its way into every area of life and translates into a big confidence boost.

\* \* \*

## *nineteen*

# Panic Never Helps

"A disciplined mind leads to happiness, and an undisciplined mind
leads to suffering."
– Dalai Lama XIV (*The Art of Happiness*)

*It's a Friday afternoon; the gym is empty except for Cory, me and our trapeze instructor, Jerry. Cory and I are doing an intensive class, with the sole purpose of working on catching and returning to the platform. For Cory, class is progressing beautifully, each of her tricks smooth and graceful, each of her returns effortless.*

*For me, not so much.*

*I'm off. Tired, possibly dehydrated and overwhelmed by life outside the gym, which is translating into a more jittery than usual trapeze class. Every little wobble in my swing, every less than perfect splits position further unnerves me. On the verge of panic, I'm completely psyching myself out.*

*By now, Jerry knows me and my flying idiosyncrasies well. "Take a break," he tells me. "Go in the other room and do five minutes of meditation. Come back when you've calmed down."*

Without tools for stilling the constant stream of thoughts, anxiety threatens my wellbeing, even with my feet firmly planted on the ground. Sitting still for meditation was almost as scary for me as flying trapeze. I had to start small. When I first began meditating, I strove for a mere two minutes per day.

We can't always stop what we're doing, however, and take a meditation break. As important as I know meditation is for my wellbeing—meditation's physical, mental, emotional and spiritual benefits are well-documented—trapeze taught me how to arrest the onset of panic without withdrawing to the proverbial Himalayan cave.

Focusing on my breath—specifically, slowing my breath down—is the easiest way I know to calm my body and mind.

In trapeze, I'll frequently notice I'm not breathing at all. In the beginning, I think I held my breath for the entire trick. Of course, that brought rigidity into my body and amplified my fear. Today when I fly, I focus on my breath as much, if not more, than any other action.

For my takeoff, I take a deep breath in as I jump up. I exhale when my body hits the 7 position, inhale to drive my legs forward, exhale as my body begins arcing backwards. I inhale to get into trick position and exhale as I release. Focusing on my breathing allows my muscle memory to take over and it takes my wacky mind out of the equation.

When I'm standing on the platform, readying myself to fly, I take long, slow, deep breaths through my nose, breathing all the way into my belly, feeling my whole body fill up with oxygen, and then exhaling all the air out through my mouth in the same slow count.

Counting my breath gives my mind one point on which to focus, which helps suspend the constant stream of thoughts that agitate my body. This deep breathing exercise can be done anytime, anywhere.

When we're in situations that cause us emotional discomfort, our human tendency is to dissociate from our bodies, which can heighten anxiety and discomfort. Another method trapeze taught me to help center myself is to focus on feeling my hands and feet.

I bring awareness to feeling my feet and how they are touching the platform or the risers before I fly. I feel how my weight is distributed. I merely observe what *is*, without trying to change anything. Connecting to my feet is, quite literally, grounding. It helps calm down the central nervous system.

Calming my mind through somatic awareness of my feet and hands, and through my breath, is a process I learn anew every day, often several times a day. I am an expert in agitating my mind. In life on the ground, I can kill my serenity in less time than it takes me to perform a trapeze trick. Negative thinking is a killer of calm. Anger, dislike, disdain, resentment, annoyance and impatience all kill my calm. Judging myself or others ruins peacefulness. Negative thoughts lead to negative feelings, negative feelings lead to negative actions, and negative actions lead to a negative, unfulfilling, unloving and unproductive life.

I've read dozens of books about affirmations, replacing the negative thoughts with positive ones, which I find helpful. Meditation and deep breathing help me integrate positive thinking.

Trapeze, for me, remains a constant reminder that my thoughts are the only things I can control. I can't always control my feelings or my body. Some days my coordination is off, my body is stiff and unyielding to my direction. But I can always gain control over my thoughts. Meditation is my chief tool for disciplining my messy mind.

\* \* \*

# *twenty*
# Everyone is a Teacher

"Every person that you meet knows something you don't; learn from them."
— H. Jackson Brown, Jr.

*It's early Tuesday morning; there are only three of us flying in today's class. The instructor, Stephan Gaudreau, a former performer with Circus Circus and owner of Trapeze Arts in Oakland, is in a creative mood and he has a goal: each of us will improve our swings. Stef instructs us in a drill he's calling the "pike-pull." Basically, we're doing pull-ups on the flying trapeze, which, for me, is even less fun than doing pull-ups on the ground. With each of my turns my hands, forearms and triceps ache, and I feel increasingly irritated with the class' rigorous routine. Exhausted, I complain that I come to class to have fun and spending most of the class doing pike-pulls, instead of bona fide tricks, is no fun at all. Stef shakes his head. "You're the only student I have who doesn't want to be taught," he says.*

*Ouch.*

*"That's not true," I stammer. "I'm taking, like, three classes a week here. How can you think I don't want to learn?"*

*I plop down on the bench as far away from Stef as I can get and pick at the calluses on my hands. Why does Stef think I show up week in and week out, driving in traffic across the Bay Bridge during business hours when I should be working, if not to learn? Of course I want to learn—I just don't get what pike-pulling myself into exhaustion is teaching me. Improving my swing is not high on my priority list. I've watched plenty of flyers spend class time working on their swings, and when it came time for the catcher to go up to his catch trap and begin catching tricks, they were too tired to make catches. Or, they hadn't warmed up their tricks and weren't prepared to make catches. For me, making catches is the most fun aspect of trapeze.*

I watched the other flyers continue the pike-pull exercise. A few classes later, something seemed different about my classmates. It took me a few weeks to realize that every one of them was swinging much higher. The pike-pull exercise had translated into a better swing. Better swings lead to better tricks and better trapeze performances. I realized then the wisdom of Stef's exercise.

More importantly, I identified a pattern that had dogged my life: I habitually dismissed potential teachers and closed myself off to an incalculable amount of information, because I wrongly judged others as having nothing to teach me.

I often dismissed Stef's instruction because he is lithe, agile, fearless—in other words, the exact opposite of me. Stef is one of the most naturally gifted flyers in the world. My assumption was that people who are naturally gifted at any skill are not as good at teaching it. Naturals are quick learners; they don't need to break skills down into tiny steps. They intuitively grasp the right way to approach their disciplines. They soar right from the start.

Because Stef couldn't relate to my fear and slow learning curve, I automatically assumed he couldn't teach me at all. My closed mind failed to recognize how closely Stef watches everyone, how accomplished he is at problem-solving, how creative—and tireless—he is at finding solutions.

I was, by far, the least accomplished trapezist among my peers at Trapeze Arts in Oakland and TrapezePro in Sonoma. My progress was painfully slow, until I realized how much I could learn by watching the other flyers closely. Paying attention showed me that each of my classmates had something I wanted and each had something to teach me. I wanted to emulate Cory's takeoff, Shannon's swing, Mitchell's moxie, Gretchen's power, Jean's grace, Hope's ease of learning, Kathy's perseverance. I knew I was fortunate because, besides the one or two instructors conducting every trapeze class, each of my fellow flyers was my teacher.

Practicing humility—that is, becoming teachable—in trapeze brought me swifter progress. I became open to every tip, trick and tidbit of advice I could receive.

I wish I could say I transferred that humility to life outside trapeze with as much ease.

On the ground, I often operated under the false premise that I was the smartest person in the room. I don't know why I developed that particular defense mechanism or character defect. I do know it was one of my least attractive and most obnoxious personality traits. It prevented me from availing myself of so much wisdom others had to offer.

Shortly after starting trapeze, I joined a meditation group (to calm my mind) that met on Saturday mornings. One group member arrived late every Saturday, walking into the meeting looking like a bag lady, her clothing disheveled, her messy hair topped off with a wacky hat.

After our group meditation period, members were invited to share about the meditation experience. Each time this woman opened her mouth, I zoned out. I had judged her as not worth listening to. I failed to recognize her as a potential teacher.

We both belonged to this group for years before I found out that she was once a principle ballerina with the San Francisco Ballet and that she continued performing in Las Vegas, Florida and locally. Moreover, she happens to be one of the most well-informed people I know and, as an activist, helped create a grassroots protest against spraying San Francisco with a toxic pesticide. Deeply spiritual, she understood and had been practicing many of the disciplines to which I had been recently introduced. I missed out on years of wisdom that she shared, because I failed to recognize her as my teacher.

Not being open to teaching can be a product of judgmentalism, ignorance or fear. I tend to shut down and close myself off from learning from others because I don't like their appearance or grammar or voice quality or some other superficiality. Or I think they're too young or too old to teach me anything valuable. I now wonder how many potential gurus I shunned because I wasn't practicing humility. I was unwilling to be teachable.

Even when I can't discern anything redeemable in someone's behavior, there is still a lesson for me—what not to do. Sometimes people who misbehave badly make the best gurus. A lousy job may teach me how not to run a business. An unpleasant encounter can teach me how not to treat others. Everyone I meet offers me an opportunity to learn and grow.

Likewise, every activity I pursue offers me lessons I can apply to all other areas of my life. Finding a passion and then pursuing it against all logical reasons not to, has taught me the most important lesson of all: without passion, life can feel like an endless stretch of gray days. Pursuing my passions brings out the colors in life. I learned this from watching others who are passionate about life. Everyone is a teacher.

\* \* \*

## twenty one

# Revel in Your Accomplishments

"The more you praise and celebrate your life, the more there is in life to celebrate."
— Oprah Winfrey

*It's two o'clock on a Sunday afternoon in early December, the first weekend after Thanksgiving and an uncharacteristically bright, sunny day for this time of year in the Bay Area. The weather, alone, is cause for celebration. As it turns out, I have even rarer, more momentous reasons to revel in this day. In honor of both my forty-fifth birthday and my accomplishments on the flying trapeze, I've invited fifty or so friends and colleagues to watch me and four friends put on a flying trapeze show.*

*Asking friends to show up for my birthday in a bad neighborhood in West Oakland on a Sunday afternoon was incredibly uncomfortable. My birthdays have always been disappointing days, falling on or within a few days of Thanksgiving. I've always felt I was competing for attention with a national holiday and the national holiday always won. Throwing myself a birthday party was unthinkable; most people would be out of town or too busy with their own families and celebrations.*

*Asking friends to show up in a bad neighborhood in West Oakland on a Sunday to watch me fly was even more uncomfortable than planning my own birthday party. There were moments while reading the "Yes" RSVPs to the Evite when I wept from the sheer intensity of my feelings.*

*Today, as I climb the ladder with fifty pairs of eyes on me, I am reaching a whole new level of nervous. I've put enormous pressure on myself to perform well. As my friends file in, fill up all the seats, spill onto the floor next to the net, or perch themselves on top of the trampoline for a better perspective, I take a few warm-up swings. I feel wonky and my timing is off—never a good sign.*

*My friend, Delfina, takes me back to the dressing room and puts her hands on my shoulders, helping to ground and calm me. She reminds me that I'm loved. I look around the room, which is filled with beautifully wrapped gifts and try to remember that my friends don't care about the results of my tricks—they're happy to support the hobby that has become my passion, the activity about which I talk incessantly. I leave the dressing room, climb the ladder again and reach out for the trapeze bar, ready for my first trick: a splits position catch to an angel return.*

*In practice, I've messed up the angel return far more times than I've done it correctly. I hear the first song from my trapeze performance playlist—Three Dog Night's "Joy to the World"—ring out. I call, "Listo," Hans calls, "Hep," and I leave the platform.*

*I perform my force out and swing into splits position. I can feel I'm not in the ideal position and I know I'm capable of much better. I hear Hans call, "Hep," and I release the bar, throwing my arms forward for him to catch me. We swing. I hear him say, "Legs up," and my body complies. Hans calls, "Hep" again, and I see my return bar, right there, where it's supposed to be. I grab the bar, sweep back with everything I have, and reach the platform. I'm extremely low, almost underneath the board, but Cory grabs my back and pulls me back up to the platform. I did it!*

There are no words to describe the feelings that pulsed through me at that moment. Even now, I'm crying, overwhelmed with emotion. That's how profound this was and still is for me. The tears are joy, pure bliss. And gratitude. I set a goal—for me, a difficult goal—and invited friends to witness the goal's accomplishment. Was it the best I've ever flown? No, but it was the most memorable. The rest of the trapeze show went by in a blur, my tricks caught and returned to the board. I had known that if I did my splits/angel well enough to safely land back on the board, the rest of my show would be gravy.

My life changed in subtle and sweeping ways after that forty-fifth birthday trapeze show. Most notably, I empowered myself. I became willing to state my intentions out loud and have them witnessed. My faith in myself grew enormously. I began to believe myself when I set a goal. Now, whenever I falter, I have fifty or so witnesses who remind me that I am capable of achieving my dreams.

The subtle changes in my life that resulted from this experience are just as important. In 1997, pre-trapeze party, I moved from New York to California, and was barely able to ask my closest friends to join me at a restaurant for dinner as a sendoff. In 2011, post-trapeze party, I left California for a year of travel through South Asia. That time, I had no qualms about gathering my closest friends at my favorite spot in San Francisco—Crissy Field, a beautiful beach along San Francisco Bay—despite it being a cold, windy day. I enjoyed a proper farewell with a meaningful ritual in a place that is significant to me. Afterwards, those who could joined me for dinner at an Indian restaurant.

Reveling in your accomplishments is as important as *accomplishing* your accomplishments. It's an act of courage to ask those you love to celebrate with you. It's also an act of generosity—it gives them permission to celebrate their own lives.

Too often we attain a long-held goal and then go right on with our warrior mindset to tackle the next goal. We don't even allow ourselves the bliss of boasting!

Through the art and discipline of trapeze I learned how to find joy in striving towards a goal and then to find ecstasy in reaping the rewards that accompany its attainment. After my trapeze show, I was on a month-long high—a pure, natural high that made me calmer, happier and more content with life. A high that was also contagious. For weeks after that performance, my friends who came out to support me called to tell me they'd begun exploring their own passions and creativity.

Celebrating yourself can be ridiculously hard. It can trigger all kinds of feelings of unworthiness, embarrassment and even shame. Celebrating yourself can inspire others to celebrate their lives, but it can also incite feelings of disdain from those who aren't able to revel in their own accomplishments and significant life events. Recently, a college friend chided me about my trapeze celebration. "Birthdays are for kids," she said.

"Says who!" I replied, reminding her she threw her husband a fiftieth birthday party.

"That's different. *I* threw him the party. *He* didn't throw it for *himself.*"

My trapeze experience taught me that if I wait for someone else to celebrate my life, I will be waiting a long time. It also taught me that I'm worthy of celebration. From the phone calls I received after my show, I know it gave others permission to revel in their own accomplishments and special days. Celebrating set a powerful example of self-love and love always creates positive energy.

Be courageous—celebrate despite disdain others may cast your way. Don't let anyone deter you from reveling in your personal accomplishments and meaningful events. Be the celebration and give others plenty of reasons to celebrate—or not—with you.

Celebrate your life. Celebrate it right now. Don't wait for your next birthday or holiday. Celebrate your life today and every day. Tomorrow is not promised and God only knows who you will inspire today.

\* \* \*

## twenty two

# Finding Your Passion

"Passion is energy. Feel the power that comes from focusing on what excites you."
– Oprah Winfrey

*I've been flying for over three years now. Hans says to me, "I love watching you fly. You always have the biggest smile on your face. When you fly, you are the happiest person I know."*

I remember the exact moment trapeze transformed from an experiment—an exercise in moving through fear and stretching far beyond my comfort zone—into passion. I'd been flying for several months and was working on my swing; my timing was terribly off, as I rushed my sweep and was late in driving my hips and legs up. I was experiencing my usual steep learning curve, fighting momentum and weightlessness, creating turbulence and sometimes bumping my butt on the platform as I attempted to muscle my way into a trick position.

And then, it happened. It just clicked. I stepped off the platform and held my position—one in which my body looks like the number 7—a nanosecond longer than usual. My sweep—a motion in which I beat both legs, straight and squeezed together, behind me—was perfectly timed. I drove my hips up, leveled off, swept again as momentum pulled my body back towards the platform and effortlessly—much to my astonishment—swung up and into splits position. I held the splits until the catcher called me off my bar and I accomplished a solid catch.

What hooked me, however, was not the swing, nor the trick, nor even the catch. It was something much less tangible. My passion for trapeze skyrocketed that day because I was one hundred percent present for the entire process. Being one with the moment brought me a form of bliss, one I'd forgotten I could experience. I left that class feeling elated, a sensation I've become quite familiar with over the ensuing years.

Passion for trapeze reawakened parts of me I'd been disconnected from for decades. It reminded me of being a teenager and awakening in the middle of the night, a short story or poem bubbling up from my subconscious, forcing me to write. That need to write, when heeded, produced bliss; a sense of timelessness, a state of being totally absorbed in the process of writing. A state of being I didn't remember knowing, until trapeze brought it back into my life.

For me, trapeze has been the perfect vehicle for transformation and reconnecting to childlike joy and discovering and rediscovering passion. Because trapeze tricks are short and trapeze, even when working on mundane skills, is exciting, I never become bored with the learning process. A trick lasts 18 seconds; my attention span is never challenged. Flying is a rush, a blast of bliss-producing dopamine. Having taken up flying trapeze during a difficult time in my life—just after the sudden death of my younger sister—trapeze gave me something outside myself and my sorrow to focus on, and the endorphins helped ease my depression. Most of all, trapeze is fun. It brought an amazing group of likeminded people into my life, a community that became my best friends.

Before trapeze, I was auditioning activities to fill the unidentified void in my life; I was searching for something to become excited about. I didn't know then that trapeze would help me become more enthusiastic about everything in my life. I look back now and realize that I was destined to fly. I had always imagined myself flying. As a child, I chased butterflies, picturing their previous lives as caterpillars and wishing there was some way for me to transform into a winged creature. Flying dreams brought joy to my sleeping hours, moments where gravity no longer existed and anything was possible. As I grew older and became firmly rooted in the ground, pragmatic and struggling to build an adult life, I forgot about my dreams of flight, that longing for complete freedom. Flying trapeze reawakened my dream, gave me wings and set my spirit free.

The greatest lesson I learned is that reconnecting to passion through the seemingly frivolous activity of flying trapeze infused other areas of my life with passion. Relationships, work and activities that no longer inspire me fell away, while new and healthier patterns have taken root. Trapeze taught me that if I want to create a life of fulfillment, fun and meaning, I must follow the path of passion.

\* \* \*

## twenty three

# Final Word: Whose Fear is It?

"The great gift of human beings is that we have the power of empathy."
— Meryl Streep

*Another trapeze class ended; I'm in my car, driving from Oakland back to my apartment in San Francisco, my senses heightened by the adrenaline high I'm enjoying. My fingers, still dusted with chalk, drum in rhythm with my singing along with Mary J. Blige. Mid-December, a North Star-like beam shimmers above the Transamerica Pyramid on this clear night, the city spreading out beyond it to the Golden Gate Bridge. Feeling a profound sense of awe and appreciation, I answer my cell phone joyfully when I see it's my dad calling. I tell him about trapeze class, that I've just learned a new skill and that after a few nasty tumbles to the net, I nailed it on the last attempt of the night without the safety lines.*

*"Oh, Lynn," his voice registers fear that immediately hits me in my chest. "Why can't you just wear the safety lines? Why do you have to make everything more dangerous than it already is? You're afraid of heights. You're going to get hurt."*

*"Take that back!" I snap, sounding like a four-year-old. "You're the scaredy-cat, not me."*

*His voice quiets, barely louder than a whisper, and then he surprises me by saying, "You're right."*

I know that some of the fear I carried from childhood into adulthood came directly from my parents. My mom is afraid of heights and, for as long as I can remember, she told me that I'm afraid of heights, too. I'm not sure this was always true, but after being told I'm fearful, repeatedly, it certainly became my truth.

My father spouted one long litany of warnings: "Don't talk to strangers. Don't trust boys. Don't wear that outfit because you can't trust boys. If you do that, you'll get hurt." I'll never forget his initial reaction when, at age twelve, I told him I wanted to join the junior high ski club: "You'll break a leg." He didn't say that to be mean, nor to ruin my experience of skiing. He said it because he felt scared. Moreover, his fear was exacerbated by the fact that I didn't seem fearful. Of course, after telling me I'd break my leg, fear took a firm hold of me. Once at the mountain, my discomfort with heights embraced my dread of getting hurt. Not surprisingly, I never managed to embrace skiing with a sense of joy and abandon.

Kids pick up on their parents' emotions. Parents, especially those lacking self-awareness, frequently project their feelings onto their children and those children grow into adults who transfer their negative feelings onto partners, friends, siblings, teachers and their own children.

When children experience feelings that are being projected by an adult who lacks self-awareness or has narcissistic tendencies, they may find it nearly impossible to discern if their feelings are truly their own, or if their feelings are merely the disowned feelings of others being pushed upon them.

Empathy is a gift. Taking on another's feelings to our own detriment, however, is a curse.

In trapeze, it can be difficult to share the platform with an inordinately fearful flyer. I know I was a drag to fly with for a long time. I was so nervous, I vibrated with fear. Now I know that I had subconsciously transferred fear onto others, a skill I learned from my parents and, I assume, they learned from theirs.

Like most trapeze skills, learning to discern whose fear was calling the shots took longer for me to learn than I care to admit. Before I realized how much fear I peddled, I first had to experience flyers who were even more fearful than I was who pushed their fear out onto others.

Today, I can become fearful in my business relationships, scared that a client won't pay me or will stop using my services. When fear and financial insecurity converge, I tend to feel angry. I also tend to project my anger onto the client. Perhaps I'll read an email and decide the client is unreasonable or difficult, or that the email has an angry tone. I'll tell myself a story that is, usually, one hundred percent fiction.

When I'm caught up in that cycle of negative emotions, I recall my trapeze experience. I claim my own feelings and allow others to have theirs. I no longer disown the uncomfortable and unattractive feelings, pushing them out onto whoever happens to be close by. Instead, I acknowledge them, sit still, listen and set them free.

Freedom, I feel, is the ultimate goal of life. Freedom from negative thinking, pain, constraints, addictions. Freedom, for me, is not about acquiring more, whether that more is knowledge, stuff or even experience. Freedom is letting go of all the crap that covers the good stuff that's already abundant in my life.

May you, too, let go of everything that holds you back. May you fly free.

\* \* \*

# Acknowledgements

I want to thank E. Katherine Kerr, Erin Reese and Marie Drennan for their insight, encouragement and guidance through the process of writing this book. I am forever grateful to everyone who coached me, caught me and taught me to fly, especially Hans Winold, Hal Anderson, Janene Davis, Stephan Gaudreau, Marek Kaszuba, Simon Rowston, Sharon Reyes, Darrell Morrow, Jake Kimball, Jennings McCown, Jerry Coughlin, Cristiano Mailhos, Chioma Onyekwere, Paris Zebadua and the instructors of Trapeze School New York. I also want to thank my fellow flyers who inspired me and demonstrated possibilities I could never have imagined before trapeze: Shannon Daily, Cory Moore, Mitchell Baker, Kat Johnston, Katie Kimball, Jean Sullivan, Jill Silver, Sue Noyes, Kathy Stulgis, Rico Dell'Osso, Siobhan Gleason, Leigh Anne Dolecki, Gretchen Turzo, A. Hope Hackett, Tracy Miller and the many other flyers at Trapeze Arts in Oakland, TrapezePro in Sonoma and Trapeze School New York. A special thanks to Jane Richey for her photography.

For a list of flying trapeze schools, visit: http://www.damnhot.com/trapeze/trapezelinks2.html.

Lynn Braz is a writer whose work has appeared in numerous publications, including *The Dallas Morning News, Philadelphia* magazine,
*Cosmopolitan* magazine, SFGate.com and *USA Today.* She is currently
writing her first novel. For more information: lynnbraz.com.

Made in the USA
San Bernardino, CA
22 March 2015